RO MOUNTAIN MAMMALS

Beginners Field Guide

Fisher • Pattie • Hartson

Edited by Krista Kagume & Wendy Pirk

PARTNERS
PUBLISHING

Contents

Reference Key

Bison (p. 8)

Mountain Goat (p. 10)

Bighorn Sheep (p. 12)

Dall's Sheep (p. 14)

North American Elk (p. 16)

White-tailed Deer (p. 18)

Mule Deer (p. 20)

Moose (p. 22)

Woodland Caribou (p. 24)

Cougar (p. 26)

Canada Lynx (p. 28)

Bobcat (p. 30)

Western Spotted Skunk (p. 32)

Striped Skunk (p. 34)

Fisher (p. 36)

American Marten (p. 38)

American Mink (p. 40)

Long-tailed Weasel (p. 42)

Short-tailed Weasel (p. 44)

Least Weasel (p. 46)

Wolverine (p. 48)

American Badger (p. 50)

North American River Otter (p. 52)

Ringtail (p. 54)

Raccoon (p. 56)

Black Bear (p. 58)

Grizzly Bear (p. 60)

Coyote (p. 62)

CARNIVORES

Gray Wolf (p. 64)

Red Fox (p. 66)

Gray Fox (p. 68)

Western Jumping Mouse (p. 70)

RODENTS

Western Harvest Mouse (p. 71)

Deer Mouse (p. 72)

Northern Grasshopper Mouse (p. 74)

Bushy-tailed Woodrat (p. 76)

Norway Rat (p. 77)

House Mouse (p. 78)

Southern Red-backed Vole (p. 79)

Western Heather Vole (p. 80)

Meadow Vole (p. 81)

Long-tailed Vole (p. 82)

Montane Vole (p. 83)

Water Vole (p. 84)

Northern Bog Lemming (p. 85)

Olive-backed Pocket Mouse (p. 86)

Ord's Kangaroo Rat (p. 87)

Northern Pocket Gopher (p. 88)

Porcupine (p. 90)

Muskrat (p. 92)

American Beaver (p. 94)

Hoary Marmot (p. 96)

Yellow-bellied Marmot (p. 98)

Columbian Ground Squirrel (p. 100)

Golden-mantled Ground Squirrel (p. 102)

Wyoming Ground Squirrel (p. 104)

RODENTS

Thirteen-lined Ground Squirrel (p. 105)

Uinta Ground Squirrel (p. 106)

White-tailed Prairie Dog (p. 108)

Least Chipmunk (p. 110)

Red-tailed Chipmunk (p. 112)

Yellow-pine Chipmunk (p. 114)

Uinta Chipmunk (p. 116)

Colorado Chipmunk (p. 118)

Red Squirrel (p. 120)

Northern Flying Squirrel (p. 122)

Abert's Squirrel (p. 124)

Rock Squirrel (p. 126)

PIKAS & HARES

American Pika (p. 128)

Snowshoe Hare (p. 130)

Black-tailed Jackrabbit (p. 132)

White-tailed Jackrabbit (p. 134)

BATS

Mountain Cottontail (p. 136)

Long-eared Myotis (p. 138)

Little Brown Myotis (p. 140)

Hoary Bat (p. 142)

Silver-haired Bat (p. 144)

Big Brown Bat (p. 146)

Townsend's Big-eared Bat (p. 148)

Spotted Bat (p. 149)

SHREWS

Dusky Shrew (p. 150)

Dwarf Shrew (p. 151)

American Water Shrew (p. 152)

Arctic Shrew (p. 153)

Pygmy Shrew (p. 154)

Desert Shrew (p. 155)

Introduction

The majestic Rocky Mountains, or Rockies, are North America's largest mountain range, stretching 3000 miles (4800 kilometres) from northern British Columbia, in western Canada, to New Mexico in the southwestern United States. This vast landscape is home to all kinds of mammals, from powerful grizzly bears and iconic bighorn sheep to tiny rodents like shrews and voles. Many of these animals are secretive and stay hidden, but they do leave signs behind as they go about their daily lives.

Everyone can learn to watch for animals and identify them. All you need is a little curiosity and awareness. Are you ready to follow the clues? Here are some common signs to look for.

Location, habitat and season

When you are watching wildlife, you should first ask yourself two questions: where am I, and what kinds of animals live here? Getting to know the geographic location and habitat that you're visiting is an important first step. No matter how hard you try, you won't see a tiger in the wild in Canada or a polar bear in the desert!

When you start exploring, find out about the area you're in and the animals that live there. Learn about the habitat, the type of landscape and the plants that grow there. For example, if you're searching for a beaver, you will need to be close to water. If you would like to see a moose in winter, a river valley is a good place to start, because it provides food and shelter. Also remember that some mammals use different habitats depending on the season and others hibernate or migrate.

Tracks and trails

Tracks are another excellent sign to watch for. The size, shape and age of tracks can help reveal which mammals have been in the area and when they passed through. River edges and lakeshores are good places to see tracks because many animals go there to drink or eat. Water also attracts carnivores, or meat eaters, who may visit drinking areas to prey on the smaller animals gathered there.

When animals use the same route often, a path will form. Paths provide clues about the animals that live in the area. Wider trails belong to larger animals such as deer, and narrower ones belong to smaller animals. For example, a well-worn path near water may form as beavers drag fresh logs to build their dam. Smaller paths near water may belong to voles, who construct trail networks to protect themselves from predators. Vole paths are about 4 in (10 cm) wide.

Burrows and dens

Just like humans, animals need a safe place to rest or shelter their young. Many animals dig underground burrows to protect themselves. Mounds of soil or holes in the ground are good signs that creatures are nearby.

Eating

When animals eat, they leave other clues. Meat-eating animals might leave bones, fur or feathers. For example, in towns or urban areas, a coyote may eat a rabbit or hare, leaving the fur behind. Plant-eating animals leave other leftovers, such as stripped bark or chewed fruit, leaves or pinecones.

Even when animals eat the same food, they eat it in different ways. For example, a squirrel will strip the scales from a pinecone, leaving it clean like a corn cob, but a woodpecker will leave the pinecone ragged or frayed.

Feces

After animals eat, they reject some parts of the food, sending it out of the body as feces (poop). Feces contains things that were not digested, such as seeds, small bones or fur. By looking at the shape, size and materials in the feces, you can tell which animal it came from and what the animal ate.

Tips for watching wildlife safely

Wildlife is fascinating to watch, but we all have a responsibility to treat animals respectfully. Here are some tips from Parks Canada to help keep both you and the wildlife safe.

1. **Learn about the area you plan to visit**, the animals that live there and what precautions you need to take.

2. **Do not feed wildlife or leave food out.** Dispose of garbage properly and keep your campsite clean. The food we eat is not healthy for wild animals, and serious problems can arise if animals become used to human food or attracted to unnatural food sources.

3. **Always keep your dog on a leash.** Did you know that off-lease dogs are one of the most common causes of wildlife attacks? Off-leash dogs can be stressful and threatening to other animals and may trigger aggressive behaviour.

4. **When you see wildlife on the roadside, slow down, stay in your car and keep moving.** Stopping on the side of the road can be dangerous, obstruct traffic and increase the risk of injury to yourself, other drivers or wildlife.

5. **Watch from a safe distance.** Stay at least 10 bus lengths (100 m or 330 ft) away from bears, wolves or cougars, and 3 bus lengths (30 m or 100 ft) away from deer, elk or moose.

6. **Travel in groups, stay together and be aware of your surroundings.** Check weather conditions before you leave. Make noise as you hike so wildlife in the area can hear you coming and have time to move away. Travel during the day because animals are most active at sunrise and sunset. Do not wear earbuds or headphones while you hike.

7. **Always stick to the trail.** Obey the signs for trail closures or restrictions to stay safe and avoid disturbing sensitive areas or wildlife.

8. **Carry bear spray** and learn how to use it, especially if large animals such as bears, wolves or cougars are present in the area you're visiting.

Mammals

Mammals are the group to which human beings belong. In general, mammals are endothermic (warm-blooded), bear live young (except for the platypus and the echidna), nurse their young and have hair or fur on their bodies. Typically, in all mammals larger than rodents, the male and the female differ in appearance, either by size or by other features such as antlers. Males are usually larger than females. Different groups of mammals include herbivores, carnivores, omnivores and insectivores.

Bison

Bison bison

Historically, millions of bison roamed much of central North America, but by the end of the 19th century, fewer than 1000 remained. Today, bison live primarily in protected areas and on private ranches.

ID: front end covered with long, shaggy dark brown hair that becomes shorter and lighter behind the shoulders; massive head appears to be carried low because of the high shoulder hump; both sexes have short, round, curved black horns that grow upward; long tail with a tuft of hair at tip; calves are reddish-brown at birth but become darker by their first autumn
Length: 8–13 ft (2.4–4 m)
Shoulder height: 4–6 ft (1.2–1.8 m)
Weight: 790–2400 lb (360–1090 kg)
Habitat: historically most abundant on the prairies, but also lived in alpine tundra and areas of boreal forest and aspen parkland with plenty of short vegetation
Diet: mostly grasses, sedges and forbs, but will browse on shrubs, cattails and lichens in winter
Group name: herd
Also called: buffalo

Bison are members of the cattle family. Like cows, they chew their cud. Bison have a complex, four-chambered stomach that helps them break down food.

The largest herd was once found in Wood Buffalo National Park in northern Alberta, Canada, where wolves and bison continue their predator-prey relationship. Today, bison are being reintroduced to other parks and conservation areas.

If bison are caught in a storm, they face into the wind, using the woolly coat of their head and shoulders to reduce the chill.

Mountain Goat

Oreamnos americanus

In winter, the mountain goat stays warm by growing a thick fleecy undercoat, topped by long guard hairs.

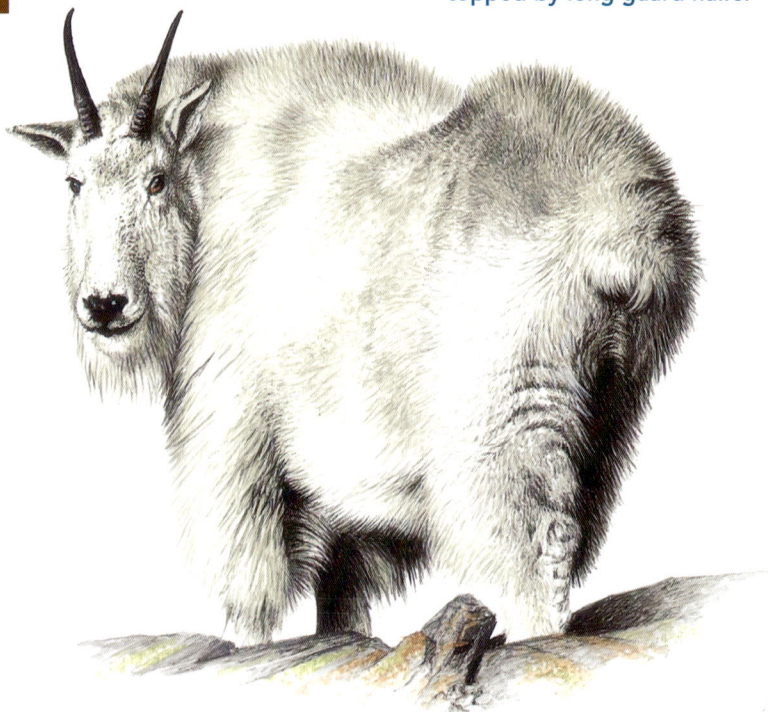

ID: stocky and hump-shouldered with a white, usually shaggy coat; black lips, nose, eyes and hooves; may have a noticeable beard, which is longer in winter; long ears; short tail; black horns are thick and curve backward on billy and are narrower and straight on nanny, curving sharply near tip
Length: 4–5 ft (1.2–1.5 m)
Shoulder height: 3–4 ft (90–120 cm)
Weight: 100–300 lb (45–135 kg)
Habitat: steep slopes and rocky cliffs in alpine and subalpine areas
Diet: shrubs, mosses, lichens, forbs, grasses, sedges, rushes
Group name: herd, band

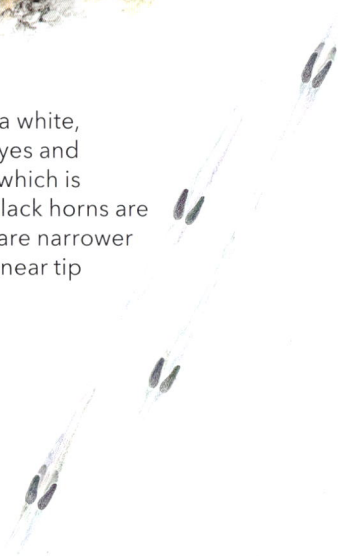

Nimble mountain goats are at home on rocky cliffs and have no fear of heights. One of the best places in the Rockies to see mountain goats is the Going to the Sun Highway in Glacier National Park, Montana.

The mountain goat has special hooves with a hard outer ring, surrounding a softer, spongy centre that provides grip on rocky surfaces. The goat can fit all four hooves on a tiny cliff ledge, 6 in (15 cm) long by 2 in (5 cm) wide, or about the size of a $5 bill. It can even rear up and turn around on such a tiny ledge.

Goats, sheep and bison are the only hoofed mammals that have true horns. These horns are never shed; they grow for the animal's entire life.

Bighorn Sheep

Ovis canadensis

The bighorn sheep is a favorite symbol of the mountain wilderness.

ID: brownish overall with a bobbed tail and large white rump patch; white belly, muzzle and inside of legs; ram's horns are thick and curve in a full curl or more; ewe's horns are shorter and thinner and curl back slightly, not even into a half circle
Length: 5-6 ft (1.5-1.8 m)
Shoulder height: 30-45 in (75-115 cm)
Weight: 120-340 lb (55-155 kg)
Habitat: unforested, mountainous areas with cliffs; steep slopes near food and water; some populations live along steep riverbanks and in gullies of desert environments
Diet: broad-leaved non-woody plants, grasses
Group name: herd
Similar species: Dall's sheep (p. 14)

Bighorn sheep are at home balancing on steep, rocky ledges. They are also commonly seen along roads in the mountain parks, where they come to lick the salt.

Adult rams go head-to-head in combat during mating season. Opposing rams rise on their hindlegs, run toward one another and smash their horns together to prove dominance.

The size of the male's horns is a symbol of rank. Dominant rams have larger horns and a bigger body.

Dall's Sheep

Ovis dalli

Dall's sheep are found in the northern regions of the Rockies, appearing as tiny, dirty spots on a northern wilderness palette. They are closely related to bighorn sheep.

ID: subspecies found in Rocky Mountains is slate brown to blackish overall; white muzzle, forehead, rump patch, and inside of hindlegs; rams have long, thick, wide-spreading, spiralled horns; ewe's horns are shorter and curve backward but never spiral
Length: $4\frac{1}{2}$–6 ft (1.4–1.8 m)
Shoulder height: 30–40 in (75–105 cm)
Weight: 100–220 lb (45–100 kg)
Habitat: alpine tundra slopes to 6560 ft (2000 m) elevation in summer; lower south or southwestern-facing slopes in winter; may travel far outside of typical habitat to find mineral licks
Diet: broad-leaved herbs in spring/summer; mostly grasses and seeds in winter, as well as willow branch tips, pasture sage and mountain avens
Group name: herd
Also called: thinhorn sheep, stone sheep
Similar species: bighorn sheep (p. 12)

Southern subspecies

There are two subspecies of Dall's sheep: the southern subspecies, sometimes called stone sheep, is the one found in the Rocky Mountains.

Northern subspecies

The northern sub-species is found in the Northwest Territories, Yukon and British Columbia, and it has a predominantly white coat.

After mating, the rams journey high into the mountains. The ewes and lambs stick to steep, rocky slopes, where there are fewer predators.

North American Elk

Cervus canadensis

The pitched bugle of the bull elk is a sign that autumn has arrived.

ID: head, neck and legs are a darker brown than rest of body; large whitish-orangey rump patch bordered by black or dark brown fur; bull has dark brown throat mane; adult bull typically has 6 points on each antler but number of points can vary
Length: 6½–8½ ft (2–2.6 m)
Shoulder height: 4–5 ft (1.2–1.5 m)
Weight: 400–1100 lb (180–500 kg)
Habitat: open forests and grasslands; sometimes ranges into coniferous forests or brushlands
Diet: sedges, grasses in spring/summer; woody plants, fallen leaves in fall/winter
Group name: herd, gang
Also called: wapiti
Similar species: moose (p. 22), mule deer (p. 20)

An adult bull starts to grow antlers at 2 years old. The antlers are shed each spring, and new ones begin to grow in late April.

In the 1800's, elk numbers dwindled, due to overhunting, prompting the Canadian government's creation of Elk Island National Park in 1906. Today, new herds have formed, thanks to conservation efforts and reintroduction programs.

Elk prefer forests and grasslands. Lush golf courses, grassy lawns and agricultural fields also provide high quality grazing areas.

White-tailed Deer

Odocoileus virginianus

White-tail deer are widespread and regularly seen in open fields and croplands.

ID: white belly, throat and underside of tail; narrow white ring around eyes; white band around muzzle; male's antlers are unbranched tines growing off the main beam. *In summer:* reddish-brown coat. *In winter:* grayish-brown coat
Length: 4$\frac{1}{2}$-7 ft (1.4-2.1 m)
Shoulder height: 2$\frac{1}{2}$-4 ft (70-120 cm)
Weight: 110-440 lb (50-200 kg)
Habitat: places with a mixture of open areas and young forest; valleys, stream courses, woodlands, meadows
Diet: forbs, grasses, some mushrooms in spring/summer; leaves, twigs in fall/winter
Group name: herd
Similar species: mule deer (p. 20)

The white-tailed deer is secretive during the daytime, remaining hidden in thick shrubs. Once the sun begins to set, it becomes active, moving gracefully to feeding areas.

This deer is named for the bright white underside of its tail, which it raises or "flags" when it is alarmed. The white flash of the tail tells other deer there is danger nearby.

This deer's nose and ears constantly twitch as it tries to sense any danger lurking nearby.

Mule Deer

Odocoileus hemionus

ID: large ears; dark forehead; dark spot on either side of nose; large whitish rump patch divided by short, black-tipped tail; white throat and underparts; male's antlers are equally branched into forked tines
Length: $4\frac{1}{2}$–$5\frac{1}{2}$ ft (1.4–1.7 m)
Shoulder height: 3–3.5 ft (90–105 cm)
Weight: 68–470 lb (30–210 kg)
Habitat: lowland coulees and dry brushland to alpine tundra in summer (bucks tend to move to higher altitudes; does and fawns remain at lower altitudes); streamside in drier regions; prefer young forest year-round
Diet: grasses, forbs in summer; leaves and twigs of shrubs in fall; twigs, woody vegetation, hay in winter
Group name: herd
Also called: black-tailed deer
Similar species: white-tailed deer (p. 18)

The mule deer has been around since prehistoric times and continues to thrive in mountains and in broken, fragmented landscapes. Mule deer frequent open areas and can be very bold, conspicuous and approachable.

The mule deer is usually silent, but it can cough, roar, grunt or even whistle. A fawn will sometimes bleat.

The mule deer is well known for its bouncing gait, called *stotting* or *pronking*. It bounds and lands on all fours at once, as if it's using a pogo stick.

Moose

Alces alces

Moose are the world's largest deer. Older bull (male) moose are easily recognizable by their large palmate antlers, though elk-like antlers are common in young bulls. Antlers are grown in spring and shed in fall or winter, and they grow back bigger every year.

ID: dark upperparts fade to lighter, often greyish lower legs; short neck with humped shoulders; bulbous nose; large dewlap or "bell" on throat; male has palmate antlers
Length: 8-10 ft (2.4-3 m)
Shoulder height: 5½-7 ft (1.7-2.1 m)
Weight: 500-1180 lb (230-540 kg)
Habitat: coniferous forests, areas with young willow and poplar trees, wetlands
Diet: twigs, branches; water plants like pondweed in summer
Similar species: North American elk (p. 16)

With its long legs, the moose can easily cross streams, step over fallen logs and walk through deep snow where predators have trouble following.

To reach water plants in summer, the moose will sink completely underwater and can stay there for up to 1 minute. It can dive to depths of 20 feet (6 m); that's about as deep as a giraffe is tall!

A female moose, called a *cow*, has 1 to 3 (usually 2) unspotted calves in late spring. To avoid wolves, cows often give birth on islands.

Woodland Caribou

Rangifer tarandus caribou

The caribou's name comes from the Mi'kmaq word *halibu*, which means "pawer" or "scratcher," and refers to the caribou's feeding strategy of digging feeding craters.

ID: medium-sized deer; mainly dark brown with creamy white neck, mane, underbelly and underside of tail; large, rounded hooves; both male and female have antlers but male's are much larger
Length: 5½–8 ft (1.7–2.4 m)
Shoulder height: 3–5½ ft (0.9–1.7 m)
Weight: 200–400 lb (90–180 kg)
Habitat: *Boreal population:* lives in northern boreal forests year-round, and occurs in most Canadian provinces and territories, from British Columbia to Newfoundland; inhabits mature coniferous forests and muskeg; sometimes moves to alpine and sub-alpine areas in summer. *Southern Mountain population:* occurs only in British Columbia and western Alberta, migrating between high and low elevation, mountainous areas
Diet: lichens, mushrooms, grasses, herbs, shrubs
Group name: herd

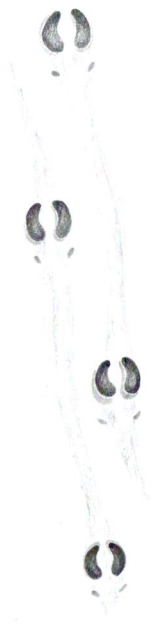

This northern specialist is better adapted to cold climates than other deer—even the caribou's nose is completely furred. Its winter coat has long, hollow guard hairs that top a fine, fleecy, insulating undercoat.

Caribou feed by digging through the snow with their broad hooves to expose lichens, their favorite winter food. Lichens grow very slowly and are often restricted to older spruce and fir forests, but a herd's erratic movements prevent overgrazing.

Caribou carve out a living in the northern forests, trekking through deep snow in winter and muskeg or black fly fens in summer. They depend on large, connected areas of wilderness as they migrate between summer and winter feeding grounds.

Cougar

Puma concolor

Cougars don't roar like lions, but they purr like housecats.

ID: large cat whose tail is more than half the length of its head and body; tawny overall with white underside; rounded head, ears and muzzle; tip of tail, sides of muzzle and backs of ears are black
Length: 5–9 ft (1.5–2.7 m)
Shoulder height: 26–32 in (66–80 cm)
Weight: 68–200 lb (30–90 kg)
Habitat: remote, wooded, rocky areas, usually far from human activity
Diet: specializes in deer and other ungulates but also preys on birds and small mammals, including beavers, porcupines, rabbits
Also called: mountain lion

Historically, cougars were found throughout most of southern Canada, with a range overlapping that of deer, their favorite prey. With the arrival of settlers, cougars were pushed westward to the foothills and mountains.

These secretive cats are not often seen. If they are around, you might see their paw prints or scratches on trees where they sharpened their claws.

The cougar is the only large, long-tailed cat in Canada. It has specialized teeth and claws for capturing prey; its sharp canines can kill a moose or deer in one lethal bite. This skilled nocturnal hunter can travel an average of 6 miles (10 km) per night.

Canada Lynx

Lynx canadensis

The Canada lynx hunts alone in remote forests. Its thick fur protects it from the bitterest cold.

ID: medium-sized cat with long legs and large feet; long black ear tufts; black stripes on forehead and long facial ruff; short, black-tipped tail
Length: 30–42 in (75–107 cm)
Shoulder height: 24–26 in (61–66 cm)
Weight: 17–26 lb (7.8–11.8 kg)
Habitat: coniferous forests with numerous fallen trees and thickets for cover and ambush sites
Diet: mostly snowshoe hares, but also squirrels, grouse, small rodents
Similar species: bobcat (p. 30)

Like other cats, the Canada lynx is not built for fast, long-distance running. Instead, it ambushes or silently stalks its prey. It is an excellent climber and often crouches on tree branches, ready to pounce on passing prey.

The secretive Canada lynx is a hunting machine. Its large, well-furred paws allow for nearly silent movement and serve as snowshoes in winter. Its bristle-tipped ears can detect the slightest sound.

Lynx populations fluctuate every 7 to 10 years with snowshoe hare numbers. When hares are plentiful, lynx kittens are more likely to survive and reproduce; when there are fewer hares, the lynx population declines.

Bobcat

Lynx rufus

The bobcat ranges from southern Canada to central Mexico, the widest distribution of any native cat in North America. It is not well adapted to deep snow and is replaced by the Canada lynx in the northern part of its range.

ID: coat has dark streaks or spots but varies from yellowish to rusty brown or gray, depending on habitat and season; dark, horizontal stripes on breast and outsides of legs; two black bars across each cheek; brown forehead stripe; ear tufts are less than 1 in (2.5 cm) long; chin, throat and undersides of tail are whitish; bobbed tail has dark barring and tip is black on top.
Length: 19–49 in (48–125 cm)
Shoulder height: 17–21 in (43–53 cm)
Weight: 15–29 lb (6.8–13 kg)
Habitat: prefers open forests and brushy areas; variety of habitats, including deserts, wetlands, occasionally in developed areas
Diet: prefers rabbit but also small rodents, squirrels, skunks, ground-nesting birds; sometimes feeds on kills of other mammals; rarely takes down larger prey like deer, pronghorn
Similar species: Canada lynx (p. 28)

The bobcat looks a lot like a large housecat, but it is a wildcat in every sense of the word. It is light footed, agile and stealthy.

A feline speedster, the bobcat can hit 30 mp/h (48 km/h) for short bursts. That's the average driving speed of a car!

Chances of seeing a Bobcat in the wild are much greater than seeing a mountain lion or Canada lynx. Bobcats seem to be more tolerant of human presence; their territories may even border on developed land.

Western Spotted Skunk

Spilogale gracilis

When threatened, the western spotted skunk stamps its feet, makes short lunges and raises its tail to warn away predators. The attacker will pay a smelly price if it ignores the warning.

ID: mainly black with a white forehead spot and four or more white stripes broken into dashes on back; pattern of white dashes is different on each individual; tail is covered with long, sparse hairs, and tip of tail is white with a black underside; small, rounded black ears; face strongly resembles a weasel's; amber eyeshine at night
Length: 9–18 in (23–46 cm)
Weight: 1½–2¾ lb (0.7–1.2 kg)
Habitat: woodlands, rocky areas, open grasslands, scrublands, farmlands; does not occupy marshlands or wet areas
Diet: omnivorous; eats mostly insects, especially grasshoppers and crickets, and berries in summer; mostly small mammals in winter
Similar species: striped skunk (p. 34)

When preparing to spray, the skunk does a handstand, arching its back and lifting its backside and tail right over its head, and then walks toward its assailant while spraying it.

This skunk is especially nimble—with surprising ease, it can climb up to holes in hollow trees or into bird nests, where it finds shelter or food.

This skunk is mainly nocturnal. To get around, it may walk, trot, gallop or make a series of weasel-like bounds.

Striped Skunk

Mephitis mephitis

The famed warning colors of skunks are so effective that they communicate their message even to people who know little or nothing else about wildlife.

ID: glossy black overall with two white stripes that run from nape down back on either side of midline and meet again at base of tail; narrow white stripe on snout extends to above eyes; white markings on tail vary in amount and distribution
Length: 21-31 in (53-78 cm)
Weight: 4$\frac{1}{4}$-9$\frac{1}{4}$ lb (1.9-4.2 kg)
Habitat: moist urban and rural habitats, including hardwood groves and agricultural areas
Diet: omnivorous; mainly eats insects; also bird eggs, nestlings, amphibians, reptiles, grains, green vegetation, carrion and, particularly in fall, small mammals, fruits, berries
Similar species: western spotted skunk (p. 32)

The striped skunk sprays in a "U" position with all four feet planted on the ground. Its noxious spray can be shot up to 20 ft (6 m), or as long as 4 park benches.

In spring and summer, striped skunks feed mainly on insects, including bees. Skunks will scratch at a hive entrance until the bees come out and then catch and chew up the bees, extracting juices, then spitting out the solid parts.

During winter, the skunk is less active, and it spends the coldest periods in communal dens.

Fisher

Pekania pennanti

Fishers are reclusive animals, about the size of a small fox. They are rarely seen, preferring intact wilderness and disappearing once development begins.

ID: back ranges from frosted gray to black; dark brown undersides, tail and legs; fox-like face with pointed snout; rounded ears are more noticeable than on other large weasels; may have a white chest spot; tail is more than half as long as body; male is typically larger than female
Length: 32–40 in (80–105 cm)
Weight: 3–13 lb (1.4–6 kg)
Habitat: dense mixed and coniferous forests; avoids open areas
Diet: opportunistic; eats small mammals, birds, berries, nuts, carrion
Similar species: American marten (p. 38)

The fisher is one of the only animals that regularly kills porcupines, expertly flipping them to gain access to the soft, unprotected belly. Amazingly, the fisher has this skill without the guidance and teachings of its parents.

Fishers have specially adapted ankle bones that allow them to rotate their feet and climb down trees headfirst.

The fisher is a good swimmer, but it rarely eats fish, preferring snowshoe hares and other small mammals.

American Marten

Martes americana

ID: light reddish-brown to dark brown body with a distinctive yellow-orange chest and throat patch; bushy tail; legs and tail are darker than head and body
Length: 22–26 in (56–66 cm)
Weight: 1 $\frac{1}{4}$–2 $\frac{3}{4}$ lb (0.6–1.2 kg)
Habitat: mature, coniferous forests that contain numerous dead trunks, branches and leaves to provide cover for its rodent prey
Diet: opportunistic; voles make up most of its diet; also small mammals, bird eggs and chicks, insects, carrion, occasionally berries, other vegetation
Also called: pine martin
Similar species: fisher (p. 36)

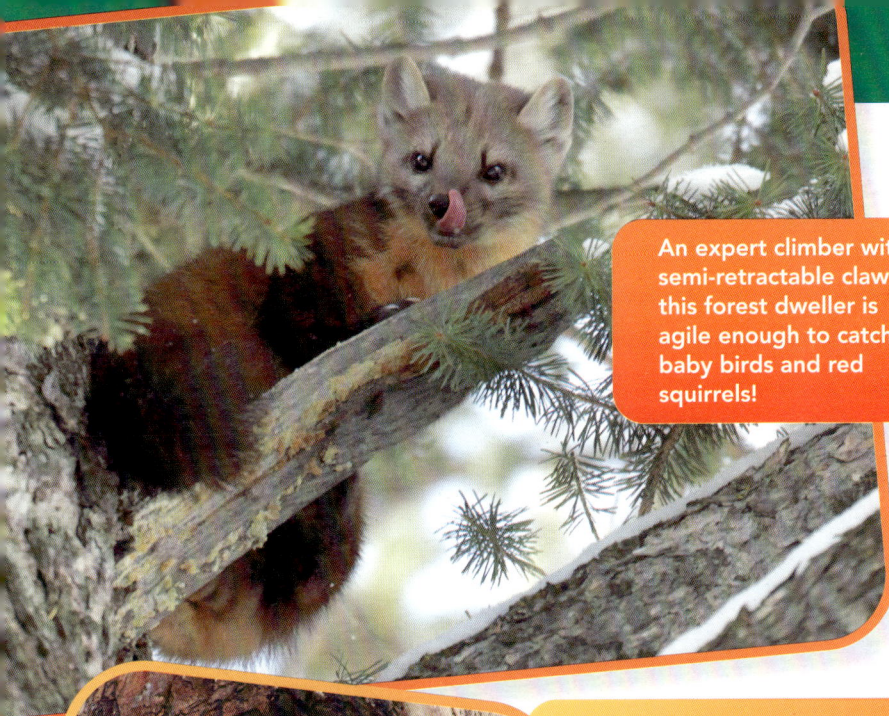

An expert climber with semi-retractable claws, this forest dweller is agile enough to catch baby birds and red squirrels!

Although it spends most of its time on the ground, the marten is equally at home among branches and tree trunks. It often dens in a tree hollow, where it raises its annual litter of up to 5 kits.

The American marten is often used as an indicator of environmental conditions because it is dependent upon food found in mature coniferous forests.

American Mink

Neogale vison

The mink's anal scent glands produce a rank, skunk-like odor.

ID: coat is generally dark brown to black, usually with white spots on chin, chest and sometimes belly; short legs; cylindrical tail, only somewhat bushy; male is nearly twice as large as female
Length: 19-26 in (48-66 cm)
Weight: 1 $\frac{3}{4}$-5 lb (0.8-2.3 kg)
Habitat: usually found near water, shorelines of lakes, marshes and streams
Diet: fierce predator of muskrats; also frogs, fish, waterfowl and their eggs, mice, voles, rabbits, snakes, crayfish, other aquatic or marine invertebrates
Similar species: American marten (p. 38), northern river otter (p. 52)

The American mink is most often seen hunting along shorelines. Its partially webbed feet make it an excellent swimmer and diver, and it often finds its food underwater.

The mink's thick, oily fur insulates the body from extremely cold waters.

Mink travel along established hunting routes, sometimes resting in a muskrat lodge after eating the original inhabitant.

Long-tailed Weasel

Neogale frenata

summer coat

ID: tail is half the length of body and has a black tip on last quarter. *In summer:* coat has cinnamon brown upperparts, orangish or buffy underparts, brown feet *In winter:* coat is white except black tail tip
Length: 13–19 in (33–48 cm)
Weight: 3–14 oz (85–400 g)
Habitat: open grassy meadows, brushland, woodlots, forest edges, fencerows
Diet: omnivorous; eats small vertebrates, insects, occasionally fruit
Similar species: least weasel (p. 46), short-tailed weasel (p. 44)

Like other mustelids, long-tailed weasels exhibit serial-killer tendencies, killing more than they can consume. Excess prey is sometimes cached for later use.

These hyperactive beasts are capable hunters that can bring down prey twice their size. In winter they hunt on or beneath the snow in tunnels.

Like other true weasels, the long-tailed turns white in winter, but the tip of its tail remains black.

Short-tailed Weasel

Mustela richarsonii

The short-tailed weasel's coat becomes white in winter, but the tail is black-tipped year-round.

summer coat

ID: short, oval ears extend noticeably above elongated head; tip of tail is black year-round; *In summer:* coat has brown upperparts, creamy white underparts and snowy white feet. *In winter:* coat is completely white
Length: 8 3/4-13 in (22-33 cm)
Weight: 1 5/8-3 3/4 oz (46-105 g)
Habitat: dense coniferous and mixed forests, shrub lands, meadows, riparian areas
Diet: small mammals, bird eggs and nestlings, insects, amphibians
Also called: ermine, stoat, American weasel
Similar species: least weasel (p. 46), long-tailed weasel (p. 42)

If short-tailed weasels were the size of black bears, we'd all be dead. These voracious, mainly nocturnal predators tend to kill anything they can take down, especially mice and voles.

A typical glimpse of this weasel is of a small, eel-like mammal bounding along then vanishing before a positive ID can be made.

The short-tailed is the Rocky Mountains most common weasel, and it may be the most abundant land carnivore.

Least Weasel

Mustela nivalis

The least weasel's tail is much shorter than those of the larger weasels.

summer coat

ID: short ears barely extend above fur; short tail may have a few black hairs at the end but never has an entirely black tip. *In summer:* walnut brown above and white below. *In winter:* white overall
Length: 6–8 $^3/_4$ in (15–23 cm)
Weight: $^7/_8$–2 $^5/_8$ oz (25–75 g)
Habitat: open fields, forest edges, rock piles, abandoned buildings
Diet: mostly mice, voles, insects; sometimes reptiles, amphibians, birds, eggs
Similar species: short-tailed weasel (p. 44), long-tailed weasel (p. 42)

If mice could talk, they would no doubt say that they live in constant fear of the least weasel. As it hunts, this miniscule barbarian charges into every hole it encounters. It is small enough to squeeze into the burrows of mice and voles.

This small, mainly nocturnal carnivore is rarely seen, but you may glimpse one dashing for cover when you move a hay bale or piece of plywood.

The least weasel eats up to its weight in food each day to fuel its incredibly fast metabolism.

Wolverine

Gulo gulo

From afar, a wolverine can look like a small brown bear, until its long, bushy tail and buffy sides are revealed.

ID: small head; arched back; long, shiny, dark cinnamon brown to nearly black coat; a buffy or pale brownish stripe runs down each side; may have yellowish-white spots on throat and chest; long legs; long, bushy tail
Length: 34–43 in (86–110 cm)
Weight: 15–35 lb (6.8–16 kg)
Habitat: large areas of remote wilderness, including forests, wooded foothills and mountains, as well as tundra
Diet: omnivorous; scavenges for carrion; also eats small animals, fish, bird eggs, berries; occasionally takes down large prey
Similar species: American badger (p. 50)

The wolverine has become a symbol of deep, pristine wilderness. Chances of seeing this elusive animal are slim, even in the most remote areas.

This muscular animal can take down a caribou or moose, but it usually scavenges carrion left behind by larger predators. With its powerful jaws, the wolverine can crunch through bone to access the nourishing marrow, leaving little trace of a carcass.

With a fondness for plastic and for marking landmarks with musk and urine, a wolverine can wreak havoc on unoccupied exploration camps.

American Badger

Taxidea taxus

Badger holes provide den sites, shelters and hibernacula for many creatures, from coyotes to black widow spiders.

ID: long, grizzled, yellowish-gray coat is longer on sides than on back; a white stripe runs from nose back onto shoulders; top of head otherwise dark; sides of face are whitish; dark vertical crescent runs between short, rounded ears and eyes; short, bottlebrush, yellowish tail; dark brown lower legs and feet become blackish at extremities
Length: 25-35 in (64-90 cm)
Weight: 11-24 lb (5-11 kg)
Habitat: open prairie and pastures, low-elevation fields, meadows, grasslands; treeless alpine slopes or riparian meadows in the mountains; alpine tundra in summer
Diet: primarily burrowing mammals; eggs, young ground-nesting birds; sometimes insects, snails, carrion, snakes
Similar species: wolverine (p. 48)

These burly, burrowing beasts are like mammalian augers. A badger at full whirl sends a continuous plume of sediment skyward, quickly disappearing underground.

Equipped with huge claws, strong forelimbs, powerful jaws and a pointed snout, badgers pursue underground prey such as ground squirrels, mice and snakes.

Badgers make an incredible variety of sounds. Adults hiss, bark, scream and snarl. In play, young badgers grunt, squeal, bark, meow, chirr and snuffle. When a badger runs on a hard surface, the front claws clatter.

North American River Otter

Lontra canadensis

Good clues to the presence of these playful creatures are "slides" on the shores of waterbodies or troughs in the snow created by tobogganing otters.

ID: large, weasel-like; dark brown upperparts look black when wet; paler below; throat is often silver gray; broad, flattened head; small eyes and ears; prominent whitish whiskers; webbed feet; long tail is thick at base and gradually tapers to tip; male is generally larger than female
Length: 3½–4½ ft (1.1–1.4 m)
Weight: 10–24 lb (4.5–11 kg)
Habitat: near wooded lakes, ponds and streams
Diet: primarily crayfish, turtles, frogs, fish; occasionally bird eggs, small mammals, insects, earthworms
Group name: bevy, romp, raft
Similar species: American beaver (p. 94), American mink (p. 40)

Playful otters often amuse themselves by rolling about, sliding, diving and bodysurfing. They especially like slippery slopes and take turns sliding down banks.

The otter's fully webbed feet, long, streamlined body and muscular tail make it a swift, effortless swimmer with incredible fishing ability.

River otters are highly social animals, usually traveling in small groups. When group of river otters travel single file through the water, their bodies form a serpent-like image—perhaps the source of rumours of lake-dwelling sea monsters.

Ringtail

Bassariscus astutus

The striking ringtail is built like a small housecat, but with a ringed tail that is as long as its body.

ID: grayish with pale underparts; pointed muzzle; long whiskers; big ears; white rings surround eyes; long, bushy tail is alternately banded black and white; tail is about same length as body
Length: 24–32 in (61–80 cm)
Weight: 1 3/4–2 1/2 lb (0.8–1.1 kg)
Habitat: rocky slopes, cliffs, canyons in southern Rockies, usually close to water
Diet: omnivorous; eats insects and other invertebrates, small mammals, reptiles, amphibians, bird eggs and nestlings, carrion, fruit
Also called: miner's cat
Similar species: raccoon (p. 56)

The ringtail is also called "miner's cat." In remote mining operations, miners appreciated the ringtail's ability to rid the premises of mice, so they put out food to encourage these nocturnal predators. The ringtails became so accustomed to sharing the food, they were almost tame.

This creature seems to have it all: it is an agile hunter and all-around athlete, and it can make a meal of almost anything digestible.

Raccoon

Procyon lotor

When on the move, raccoons are easily recognizable by their hunchbacked appearance.

ID: long, grizzled, blackish to brownish-gray coat; lighter underparts; similar in size to a large, fat housecat; bushy tail has 4–6 dark rings; distinct black "mask" across eyes bordered by white "eyebrow"; mostly white snout; small ears
Length: 26–37 in (66–95 cm)
Weight: 12–31 lb (5.4–14 kg)
Habitat: wooded areas near water; urban areas
Diet: omnivorous; fruits, nuts, berries, insects, clams, frogs, fish, eggs, young birds, rodents; also human food
Similar species: ringtail (p. 54)

These intelligent, black-masked bandits are common in many habitats, including suburbia. They are well known for looting people's gardens, cabins, campsites and even garbage cans.

While not a true hibernator, raccoons become sluggish during colder weather and may hole up for extended periods. These agile climbers are often seen high in trees or peeking from arboreal cavities.

Raccoons are known for wetting their food before eating, a behavior that allows them to feel for and discard any inedible matter.

Black Bear

Ursus americanus

Black bears are usually shy and prefer forested areas, but they may wander into urban areas searching for something to eat. Bears have good memories and will return to food sources, such as fruit trees or garbage.

ID: long, shaggy coat can be black or brown to cinnamon or honey-colored; light-colored muzzle; evenly sloping facial profile; short, stout body; short, powerful legs; large, wide feet with curved black claws
Length: 4½–6 ft (1.4–1.8 m)
Shoulder height: 3–3½ ft (0.9–1.1 m)
Weight: 88–595 lb (40–270 kg)
Habitat: forests and open, marshy woodlands or riparian areas throughout most of North America; alpine meadows and avalanche slopes in the mountains; avoids grasslands and deserts
Diet: fruit, berries, other vegetation; insects including larvae and grubs; small mammals, fish, eggs, carrion
Similar species: grizzly bear (p. 60)

Contrary to popular belief, black bears do not usually hunt larger animals. These opportunistic foragers feed on whatever food is easy and abundant. Thier molar teeth are very similar to those of humans.

During its winter slumber, a black bear loses 20 to 40 percent of its body weight. To prepare for winter, the bear must eat thousands of calories a day during late summer and fall.

Wildlife overpasses allow bears and other animals to move over busy highways in Banff National Park, Canada. These bridges effectively open migration corridors and save countless animals from vehicle collisions.

Grizzly Bear

Ursus arctos

A grizzly will enter its den to hibernate in late October or November during a heavy snowfall that will cover its tracks.

ID: prominent shoulder hump; dished face; pale yellow to dark brown coat; long front claws are always visible
Length: 6–8½ ft (1.8–2.6 m)
Shoulder height: 3–4 ft (0.9–1.2 m)
Weight: 240–1160 lb (110–530 kg)
Habitat: forests and riparian areas
Diet: omnivorous; mostly plants, carrion; also fish, insects, small mammals, bighorn sheep
Also called: brown bear
Similar species: black bear (p. 58)

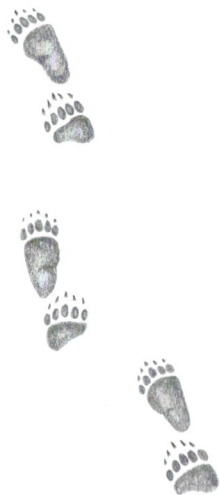

A mother grizzly with cubs can be very dangerous. Hikers are advised to practice bear safety techniques and carefully stow all food.

Grizzly bears are incredibly strong and can roll huge rocks to get at the insect underneath, drag elk carcasses and crush thick bones. However, they spend much of their time munching on roots, berries and grasses.

Adult grizzlies cannot easily climb trees, because their claws are typically blunt from digging. If you think you can escape one by climbing a tree, though, you better climb high because grizzlies can stand on their hind legs and reach well up a tree.

Coyote

Canis latrans

Coyotes are intelligent, curious and adaptable.

ID: gray, buffy or reddish-gray, medium-sized dog; nose is pointed; usually a gray patch between eyes that contrasts with rufous top of snout; bushy tail has a black tip; underparts are light to whitish
Length: $3\frac{1}{2}$–$4\frac{1}{2}$ ft (1.1-1.4 m)
Shoulder height: 23-26 in (58-66 cm)
Weight: 18-44 lb (8.2-22 kg)
Habitat: open woodlands, agricultural lands, near urban areas; often range into suburbia and even live in densely populated cities
Diet: rodents, rabbits, birds, amphibians, reptiles, insects, plants; scavenges for food; may take exposed calves, sheep, chickens
Group name: pack
Similar species: gray wolf (p. 64)

Coyotes live in many climates and habitats, often close to humans, and have thrived with the expansion of agriculture and forestry.

Coyotes and wolves look similar, but coyotes are usually smaller and have a slimmer snout. The coyote drags its tail behind its legs when it runs.

They occasionally form loose packs and join in spirited yipping choruses. Listen for their whines, barks and howls at sunset.

Gray Wolf

Canis lupus

Gray wolves are the world's largest wild dogs. They are crucial to a healthy, balanced ecosystem.

ID: typically gray overall, but coat can range from coal black to creamy white; black wolves are most common in dense forests; whitish wolves are characteristic of the high Arctic; carries its bushy tail straight behind it when it runs
Length: 4½–6½ ft (1.4–2 m)
Shoulder height: 26–38 in (66–100 cm)
Weight: 57–170 lb (26–77 kg)
Habitat: mainly found in forests, mountains, riparian areas and Arctic tundra
Diet: mainly large mammals such as deer and bighorn sheep; also rabbits, mice, nesting birds, carrion when available
Group name: pack
Also called: timber wolf
Similar species: coyote (p. 62)

Wolves are famous for howling. They howl to stay in touch with the pack, begin a hunt or keep other wolves out of their territory.

Wolves are social animals that live in groups called *packs*.

Wolf packs cooperate within a strong social structure that is dominated by an alpha pair (dominant male and female). Order and status are reinforced with a complex mix of body language, facial expressions and vocalizations.

Red Fox

Vulpes vulpes

Tracks are often the best sign foxes are present: their small, oval prints form a nearly straight line.

ID: typically rusty, reddish-brown overall, but variations include blackish and even a silvery form
Length: 35–44 in (90–110 cm)
Shoulder height: 16 in (40 cm)
Weight: 8–15 lb (3.6–6.8 kg)
Habitat: open habitats with brushy shelter, riparian areas, edge habitats
Diet: opportunistic; mostly small rodents, rabbits and birds but also dried berries in winter; invertebrates, birds, eggs, fruits, berries in more moderate seasons

These small animals look like dogs but often act like cats: they stalk mice and other small prey and make energetic pounces to capture victims. The fox's bushy tail provides balance when running or jumping.

Foxes are playful in their natural habitat. Young fox kits wrestle and squabble together or amuse themselves by playing with a stick or old bone.

Cleverness and cunning have long been associated with foxes, giving rise to the old saying, "as crafty as a fox."

Gray Fox

Urocyon cinereoargenteus

The gray fox is the only North American member of the dog family that can climb.

ID: grizzled appearance, with long, grayish fur over its back; reddish underparts, back of head and throat, legs and feet; belly mostly white with reddish highlights; long tail with a black tip; pointed ears; distinct black spot on either side of muzzle
Length: 31-44 in (78-110 cm)
Shoulder height: 14-15 in (36-38 cm)
Weight: 7½-13 lb (3.4-6kg)
Habitat: prefers rocky, shrub-covered terrain, always near trees or groundcover
Diet: omnivorous; small animals such as rabbits, rodents, birds; also insects, other invertebrates, plants, including fruits, grasses, apples, nuts

Truly a crafty fox, the gray fox is most remarkable for its ability to climb trees to escape danger, find egg-filled nests or rest. It may also use a natural tree cavity for denning.

Although this fox is quite small, it can run very quickly over short distances. In one record, a gray fox topped 28 mph (45 km/h), almost as fast as a car drives in the city.

The gray fox has suffered less persecution from farmers because it is quite shy and not inclined to take domestic animals such as chickens. It prefers to hunt mice.

Western Jumping Mouse

Zapus princeps

This mouse is a great digger, swimmer and jumper. When facing danger, it uses its large back legs and long tail to leap to safer ground. It also swims well and can dive underwater.

This secretive mouse is rarely seen. It is usually active at night, foraging for seeds and the occasional insect.

Before hibernating, this mouse will nearly double its weight, then snuggle up in a ball of grass at the back of a burrow. Jumping mice spend up to eight months of the year in hibernation, one of the longest periods of any North American mammal.

ID: dark clay-colored dorsal stripe runs from nose to rump; yellowish-olive sides with orangish hairs; creamy white belly; long, naked tail is olive brown above and whitish below; hindfeet greatly elongated
Length: 7-10 in (18-25 cm)
Habitat: prefers areas of tall grass, especially along streambanks and marshes; ranges from valley floor to treeline and even into tundra meadows in mountains
Diet: berries, insects, invertebrates in spring/summer; grass seeds, fruit, fungi in fall

Western Harvest Mouse

Reithrodontomys megalotis

The western harvest mouse does not store food in any great quantities, which is understandable for an animal that usually lives for less than a year.

The harvest mouse is named for its habit of collecting grasses in mounds along its network of trails.

Ball-shaped nests are woven from grass and lined with soft plant down. Amazingly, females may produce up to 14 litters in a single year, each averaging 4 young per litter!

ID: small head; pointed nose; short gray to brown pelage with white to gray undersides; dark band down length of back; long, bicolored tail
Length: $4\frac{1}{4}$-6 in (11-15 cm)
Habitat: grasslands, meadows, fields, fence lines, riparian areas with scattered shrubs and forbs
Diet: seeds, insects; green vegetation or grass cuttings in spring/early summer
Similar species: house mouse (p. 78)

Deer Mouse

Peromyscus maniculatus

The deer mouse is named for its similarity in coloring to that of the white-tailed deer.

ID: gray to dark reddish-brown above; white undersides and feet; protruding eyes; large ears; distinctly bicolored tail
Length: 5½– 8¼ in (14–21 cm)
Habitat: various habitats including prairie grasslands, mossy depressions, brushy areas, tundra, heavily wooded areas, buildings
Diet: seeds, nuts, berries, vegetation, insects. spiders, caterpillars, fungi, flowers, carrion, bird eggs; will also raid your pantry
Also called: North American deer mouse
Similar species: house mouse (p. 78)

To even the most committed mouse-o-phobe, the deer mouse looks cute. Its large, dark eyes give it a curious look, while its dainty nose and continuously twitching whiskers sense changes in the wind.

This mouse is a great climber and often nests in trees cavities, hollow logs, old buildings or bluebird nest boxes, building a dense nest of plant matter. Unlike most mammals, the male deer mouse often helps the female raise their young.

Northern Grasshopper Mouse

Onychomys leucogaster

This mouse has naturally oily fur and keeps clean by taking dust baths.

ID: gray to yellowish buff back; white belly; large ears; short, thick tail is dark above and white below with a white tip
Length: 5-6 in (13-15 cm)
Habitat: a variety of open habitats with sandy or gravelly soils, from grasslands to sandy brushlands
Diet: mostly insects, especially grasshoppers; also scorpions, small mammals, birds; some seeds and vegetation, mostly in winter
Similar species: deer mouse (p. 72)

True to its stocky form, the northern grasshopper mouse has a predatory nature. Up to 90 percent of its diet consists of animals, primarily insects but also mammals and birds up to 3 times its own weight.

The northern grasshopper mouse can produce complex vocalizations. Mated pairs hunt simultaneously, and they apparently keep in contact with frequent bird-like calls that can be heard 100 yards (90 m) away.

This mouse usurps the homes of other small mammals and modifies their burrows to suit its own needs.

Bushy-tailed Woodrat

Neotoma cinerea

The bushy-tailed woodrat, sometimes called a "packrat," is infamous for collecting objects, including twigs, bones, pine cones, bottle caps, rings, pens and coins.

When a very old woodrat nest in an old cabin near the Banff Springs Hotel was torn apart some years ago, a collection of hotel silverware dating back to the earliest days of the hotel was found.

This animal is also sometimes called a "trade rat," often trading an object in its mouth for a more attractive item.

Bushy-tailed woodrats tend to nest in rocky areas, making massive, messy nests. Rival males fight fiercely over suitable, secure nest sites. Several females may be found nesting with a single male.

Woodrats are most active after dark. They use their long whiskers to feel around in the darkness of caves, mines and the night.

ID: gray, pale pinkish or grizzled brown back; white belly; long, soft, dense, buffy fur underlain by a short, soft underfur; large, protruding, black eyes; big, fur-covered ears; long, abundant whiskers; long, bushy, almost squirrel-like tail is gray above and white below
Length: 11–18 in (28–46 cm)
Weight: 2 $\frac{3}{4}$–18 oz (80–510 g)
Habitat: rocks, shrubs, abandoned buildings, mine shafts, caves
Diet: primarily leaves of shrubs; also conifer needles, seeds, berries, mushrooms, roots, bulbs; stores food in caches for winter
Similar species: American pika (p. 128)

Norway Rat

Rattus norvegicus

Native to Europe and Asia, Norway rats came to North America as stowaways on early ships. They travelled inland by hitchhiking a ride on trucks or trains.

Mountainous and northern regions are largely inhospitable to rats, but they may be found in developed areas and near human settlements.

Females can have several litters per season, each with 6 to 22 babies. The babies are born blind and don't open their eyes until they are about 10 days old.

Although they can, Norway rats seldom dig long burrows. They prefer to nest in a cavity scratched under a floorboard or the space beneath an abandoned building.

ID: brown to reddish-brown, often grizzled pelage with gray tones and grayish undersides; pale belly; long, rounded, tapered tail is darker above and lighter below; large ears, covered with short, fine hairs
Length: 12–18 in (30–46 cm)
Weight: 7–17 oz (200–480 g)
Habitat: nearly always found close to human habitation including urban areas, farmyards, abandoned buildings, garbage dumps; away from people they prefer thickly vegetated areas
Diet: grains, fruits, vegetation, insects, carrion, garbage
Also called: brown rat, common rat, sewer rat, water rat
Similar species: bushy-tailed woodrat (p. 72), muskrat (p. 92)

House Mouse

Mus musculus

House mice are gregarious and social, even grooming one another.

Like the Norway rat, the house mouse arrived as a stowaway on ships from Europe, quickly spreading across the continent alongside European settlers.

Chances are, if you have a mouse in your house, it is a house mouse. These widespread animals are found in most countries around the world.

In fact, the house mouse's dispersal closely mirrors the agricultural development of humans.

ID: yellowish-brown to blackish-gray back; gray undersides; large, almost hairless ears; long tapered, hairless tail
Length: 5–8 in (13–20 cm)
Habitat: usually associated with human settlements, including houses, garages, farms, garbage dumps, granaries
Diet: mainly seeds, stems, leaves; also eats insects, carrion, human food
Similar species: western harvest mouse (p. 71), deer mouse (p. 72)

Southern Red-backed Vole

Clethrionomys gapperi

Though it is active both day and night, this vole is almost never seen. It scurries on its short legs through almost invisible runways on the forest floor.

Like other voles, it does not hibernate during winter; instead, it tunnels around the subnivean layer—along the ground, under the snow—in search of seeds, nuts and leaves.

This vole makes its summer nest in shallow burrows, rotten logs or rock crevices. Its winter nest is subnivean.

ID: reddish-brown back on an otherwise grayish body; grayish feet; black eyes; slightly pointed nose; round ears; short slender tail is scantily haired
Length: 4 $\frac{3}{4}$–6 $\frac{1}{4}$ in (12-16 cm)
Habitat: mixed-wood and coniferous forests, bogs, riparian areas
Diet: seeds, nuts, leaves, berries, lichens, fungi
Similar species: meadow vole (p. 81), long-tailed vole (p. 82), western heather vole (p. 80)

Western Heather Vole

Phenacomys intermedius

The heather vole is named for its alpine and tundra habitats, where heathers are common.

Gnaw marks at the bottom of willow or birch provide evidence of this vole's presence.

This vole eats a high percentage of bark seasonally, and it has a cecum (a functional appendix) that assists in digesting this fibrous and lignin-rich food.

Heather voles generally occupy alpine tundra, but they may descend to northern woodlands, where their skulls are often found in owl pellets.

ID: dark brown to grayish-brown above; round ears barely extend above fur; silvery undersides; white feet; short, thin, bicolored tail
Length: $4\frac{1}{4}$–$6\frac{1}{4}$ in (11–16 cm)
Habitat: prefers open areas in coniferous forests, mountain meadows, talus slopes with evergreen herbs and shrubs, alpine tundra
Diet: heaths such as kinnikinnick, as well as bark of willow; grasses, bark, leaves, lichen, seeds, fungi, berries in summer
Similar species: southern red-backed vole (p. 79)

Meadow Vole

Microtus pennsylvanicus

Primarily active at night, this common vole can occasionally be seen in the daytime along fence lines, in agricultural fields and in urban meadows.

As a response to high predation rates, meadow voles are ready to breed 3 to 4 weeks after birth.

A complex network of grass-covered runways remaining on a meadow surface after the spring thaw is evidence of the busy meadow vole. Highways, chambers and nests, previously buried beneath the snow, are exposed to the world.

ID: blackish-brown above with gray undersides; small, black protruding eyes; rounded ears mostly hidden in long fur of rounded head; tops of feet are blackish-brown; tail is about twice as long as hindfoot
Length: 5–8 in (13–20 cm)
Habitat: alpine tundra, taiga, deciduous forests, open plains, cultivated fields, around marshes, waterbodies, areas with dense herbaceous shrubs
Diet: sedges, grasses, forbes in summer; seeds, bark, insects in winter; also eats ground beans, grains, roots, bulbs
Also called: field mouse
Similar species: montane vole (p. 83)

Long-tailed Vole

Microtus longicaudus

Long-tailed voles are found only in the mountainous areas of western North America and are essential members of the Rocky Mountain ecosystems.

These voles usually live in wet meadows with stunted thickets. They do not follow well-defined trails, and they range widely at night.

ID: dark gray to brown upperparts; black guard hairs may give a dark appearance; pale gray undersides; long, indistinctly bicolored tail
Length: 7-9 in (18-23 cm)
Habitat: variety of habitats, including dry grassy areas, mountain meadows, coniferous forests, alpine tundra near water
Diet: green leaves, grass shoots, fruits, berries in summer; bark of heaths, willows and trees in winter
Similar species: southern red-backed vole (p. 79)

Montane Vole

Microtus montanus

When the sun sets in the Rocky Mountains, the forest comes alive with rustling leaves and the scurrying footsteps of voles.

Favorable environmental conditions may allow montane voles to reproduce to brief densities of 10,000 to 30,000 voles per hectare!

This vole shares many habits and habitat preferences with the more widely distributed meadow vole, but it is rarely found where the meadow vole is established.

ID: small, thickset animal; grizzled brown to gray overall; lighter, gray-white undersides; rounded head with small, rounded ears and blunt snout; appears short-legged; long bicolored tail sparsely covered with hair
Length: 5–7 in (13–18 cm)
Habitat: a variety of habitats at various elevations, including alpine tundra and grassy mountain meadows; usually wherever meadow vole is absent
Diet: primarily green, grassy shoots when available; also seeds, bark
Similar species: meadow vole (p. 81)

Water Vole

Microtus richardsoni

An excellent swimmer and diver, the water vole is like a small alpine muskrat in many ways. It lives along streams and has dense, water-repellent underfur that insulates its body from the cold water.

To avoid predators, the water vole builds extensive networks of burrows, often with direct entrances into water.

Few water voles live beyond 1 year, falling prey to weasels, hawks, owls, snakes and foxes.

ID: large, blackish-brown body with gray sides; grayish-white undersides; long hindfeet; indistinctly bicolored tail
Length: 9–11 in (23–28 cm)
Habitat: along alpine and sub-alpine streams and lakes
Diet: sedges, grasses, roots, flowers, other vegetation in summer; bark of willows and bog birch, roots, fruits, seeds in winter
Also called: North American water vole

Northern Bog Lemming

Synaptomys borealis

A fleeting view of a brown ball of fur racing through the hummocky ground of a sphagnum bog may be your only sight of this busy rodent.

The northern bog lemming maintains an extensive network of mossy runways year-round that are frequently marked by evenly clipped grass in neat piles.

Like most other small mammals, this lemming remains active throughout winter and is an important source of food for many predators.

ID: stout body covered in thick fur; sides and back usually chestnut or dark brown; underparts usually grayish; patch of tawny hair just behind ears; ears barely project above fur
Length: 4½– 5½ in (11-14 cm)
Habitat: wet alpine tundra, lake borders, sphagnum bogs, black spruce forests with Labrador tea and moss
Diet: mainly sedges, grasses
Similar species: long-tailed vole (p. 80), meadow vole (p. 81)

Olive-backed Pocket Mouse

Perognathus fasciatus

Considered the slowest of all rodents, this pocket mouse spends much of the day grooming itself in an underground burrow but becomes active at dusk.

This tiny rodent moves in an unusual hop, using all 4 limbs. When threatened, it will explode into motion, leaping very high.

Unlike hibernating rodents, pocket mice do not build up a store of fat. Instead, they pack their burrows with vast numbers of seeds.

Pocket mice do not need to drink water. Their metabolism generates water through the digestion of lipids in the oily seeds they eat.

ID: tiny mouse; back is buffy with olive or blackish hairs; lighter sides and underparts; long, thin tail is uniformly coloured
Length: (4–6 in) 10–15 cm
Habitat: open, active sand dunes and thinly vegetated grasslands of southeastern Alberta south to Colorado
Diet: seeds with a higher than average oil content such as thistle, knotweed, bluegrass or lamb's-quarters; also green vegetation, insects
Similar species: Ord's kangaroo rat (p. 87)

Ord's Kangaroo Rat

Dipodomys ordii

Powerful hind legs and a long, muscular tail give this endearing little creature the ability to leap up to 8 ft (2.4 m) in a single hop. That is the length of a couch!

Mainly a nocturnal granivore this kangaroo rat forages for seeds and the occasional plant or insect by night, while resting in its short, sandy burrow by day.

The kangaroo rat rarely drinks water, getting most of the liquid it needs from food and internally recycled wastes.

ID: orange-brown overall; white underbelly; white spot above eye and behind ear; white line across hip; tail has tufted end and is at least as long as body; long hindfeet; greatly reduced forelegs are held up as animal stands on hindlegs
Length: 9–11 in (23–28 cm)
Habitat: grasslands, shrublands, sand dunes, open areas with sandy soils
Diet: mainly seeds year-round; some insects in spring; grasshoppers, roots in summer
Similar species: olive-backed pocket mouse (p. 86)

Northern Pocket Gopher

Thomomys talpoides

This highly adapted rodent has long front claws for digging and furred lips that extend over the long incisor teeth to prevent dirt from entering its mouth. Its fur-lined cheek pouches are used to temporarily store succulent roots, tubers and green plants.

ID: squat, bullet-headed rodent with visible incisors; upperparts are slightly darker than underparts and often match soil color; long foreclaws; thick, nearly hairless tail; a row of stiff hairs surrounds naked soles of forefeet
Length: 7½–10 in (19–25 cm)
Habitat: mountain meadows, fields, shrublands, grasslands, open pine forests
Diet: succulent underground plant parts are staple diet; may emerge at night to collect green vegetation in summer

This pocket gopher spends most of its life underground but occasionally tunnels to the surface at night to find lush, green plants, leaving dirt mounds at the surface. In many agricultural areas, it is the most controlled "nuisance" mammal because of these mounds, which can damage machinery and cover vegetation.

The northern pocket gopher is one of nature's rototillers. This ground-dwelling rodent continually tunnels through dark, rich soils, and an individual can turn over 33,000 lb (15,000 kg) of soil every year—or about the weight of an elephant.

Porcupine

Erethizon dorsatum

A porcupine's quills are modified stiff hairs with overlapping, shingle-like barbs on their tips.

ID: large, stout-bodied rodent with long, light-tipped guard hairs on back and long, thick quills; young mostly black but adults may be tinged with yellow; top of thick tail has dark-tipped, white to yellowish quills; sharp, curved front claws
Length: 21–37 in (53–95 cm)
Weight: 7½–31 lb (3.4–14 kg)
Habitat: ranging from coniferous and mixed deciduous-coniferous forests to open tundra and rangelands
Diet: completely herbivorous; eats leaves, buds, twigs, young bark and sugary cambium layer of trees; also forbs, shrubs, other vegetation
Also called: North American porcupine

Contrary to popular belief, a porcupine cannot throw its 30,000 or so quills, but it does rely on a lightning-fast flick of the tail to deliver the quills into persistent attackers.

Porcupines are excellent tree climbers, using their sharp curved claws, feet and tail to climb. Missing patches of bark are a sign of porcupine activity. They can move far out on thin branches to eat young, tender bark.

Their insatiable craving for salt occasionally drives porcupines to gnaw on rubber tires, wooden ax handles, toilet seats in outhouses and even hiking boots!

Muskrat

Ondatra zibethicus

Although it looks like a small, skinny-tailed beaver, the muskrat is actually a member of the vole family.

ID: long, shiny, tawny to nearly black guard hairs overlay brownish-gray undercoat; lighter flanks and sides; gray underparts with tawny guard hairs; long, black, nearly hairless tail is scaly and laterally compressed; large, partially webbed hindfeet; long, strong claws
Length: 1½–2 ft (48–61 cm)
Weight: 1¾ lb–3½ lb (0.8–1.6 kg)
Habitat: lakes, marshes, ponds, rivers, reservoirs, dugouts, canals with cattails and rushes; may be found in urban stormwater ponds
Diet: emergent herbaceous vegetation, such as cattails, rushes, sedges and pondweed, frogs, turtles, snails, crayfish in summer; submerged vegetation in winter
Also called: common muskrat
Similar species: American beaver (p. 94), Norway rat (p. 77)

Muskrats construct open-water canals, creating habitats for many species of waterfowl and aquatic plants that could not otherwise survive in dense stands of cattails and sedges.

Muskrat houses are domed heaps of mud, cattails and rushes, surrounded by water. The houses are built entirely of aquatic vegetation and have an underwater entrance.

Muskrats spend the long winter swimming and feeding beneath the ice. They do not venture to the world above until the first few weeks of spring.

American Beaver

Castor canadensis

The loud slap of a beaver's tail on water warns of intruders.

Beavers can remain under water for up to 15 minutes. Their broad, flattened tail is an extremely effective propulsion device.

ID: large, dark brown body; broad, flat, scaly tail; broad head with short ears; massive, protruding, orange-faced incisors; webbed hindfeet
Length: 3-4 ft (0.9-1.2 m)
Weight: 35-68 lb (16-30 kg)
Habitat: lakes, ponds, marshes, slow-flowing rivers, streams
Diet: favors bark and cambium, particularly that of aspen, willow, alder and birch; also aquatic pond vegetation in summer; occasionally eats grains, grasses
Similar species: muskrat (p. 92)

Beavers skillfully construct and maintain their dams and lodges. They are one of the few mammals that significantly alter habitat to suit their own needs.

When beavers dam a creak, they set in motion ecological succession. The upstream lowlands flood, creating changes in vegetation and favorable habitat for waterfowl, fish, insects, muskrats and other animals.

Beavers' long, continuously growing front incisors are perfect tools for gnawing down trees. Shrubs and fallen trees serve as both food and building materials.

Hoary Marmot

Marmota caligata

These stocky alpine sentinels pose on boulders, gazing for hours at the surrounding mountain scenery. Marmots usually emerge from their burrows at sunrise but remain hidden on windy, stormy days.

This marmot gives a shrill, resounding whistle, giving it the nickname "whistler."

ID: stocky and short-legged; mainly gray overall with a darker face and lower back; white nose patch; short, rounded, dark ears; dark brown feet; bushy, brown to reddish tail
Length: 27–32 in (69–80 cm)
Weight: 11–15 lb (5–6.8 kg)
Habitat: rocky subalpine slopes, rockslides, alpine meadows
Diet: plants, including grasses, sedges, broad-leaved herbs
Similar species: yellow-bellied marmot (p. 98)

Marmots have few predators but will fall prey to golden eagles, grizzlies and wolverines. When alarmed, marmots scramble over rocks and through boulder fields, to one of their many escape tunnels.

When all else fails...sleep! That's the hoary marmot's strategy for surviving in its harsh, high alpine environment. A marmot hibernates from 5 to 9 months each year from late fall to early spring.

This marmot often fails to groom its lower back, tail and hindquarters, so the fur there appears matted and rumpled.

Yellow-bellied Marmot

Marmota flaviventris

Counting hibernation and nighttime sleep, yellow-bellied marmots spend about 80 percent of their lives in their burrows.

ID: dark head with yellowish band across bridge of nose; short, rounded ears; dark, prominent whiskers; tawny or yellow-brown back with light-tipped guard hairs; bright, buffy-yellow belly, sides of neck, upper jaw and hips; blackish-brown feet and legs; dark, grizzled, bushy tail; often arches tail and flags it from side to side
Length: 19–26 in (48–66 cm)
Weight: 3½–11 lb (1.6-5 kg)
Habitat: rocky subalpine slopes and outcroppings close to a source of grassy or herbaceous vegetation
Diet: abundant herbaceous or grassy vegetation must be available within a short distance of den; occasionally feeds on road-killed carrion
Similar species: hoary marmot (p. 96)

Yellow-bellied marmots excavate a network of burrows under the rocky terrain to find shelter from freezing temperatures, strong winds and predators such as golden eagles, mountain lions and grizzly bears.

These marmots live in harem colonies and bask in the sun on warm summer days.

These marmots like their dens to be kept clean. When they emerge from hibernation, they throw out their used bedding and replace it with fresh grass and leaves, then continue to clean their burrows all summer long.

Columbian Ground Squirrel

Urocitellus columbianus

Columbian ground squirrels have been known to hibernate for up to 220 days.

ID: cinnamon-buff overall, with black-tipped guard hairs giving a dappled, black-and-buffy effect; top of head, nape and sides of neck are rich gray, with black overtones; buffy eye ring; tawny nose and face; moderately bushy, brownish-black tail; tail hairs have buffy-white tips
Length: 13–15 in (33–38 cm)
Weight: 16–20 oz (450–570 g)
Habitat: sagebrush, fields and montane meadows at mid- to high elevations
Diet: a variety of foods including herbaceous plants, grasses, insects, birds, eggs, small vertebrates
Similar species: yellow-bellied marmot (p. 98)

These robust, sleek and colorful animals chirp loudly, often at the first sight of anything unusual, and issue loud trills.

During hot, dry spells, ground squirrels estivate (a dormant state similar to hibernation) to conserve energy.

From montane valleys to alpine meadows, the Columbian ground squirrel is a common sight in mountainous regions and is often seen at heavily visited day-use areas and campgrounds.

Golden-mantled Ground Squirrel

Callospermophilus lateralis

This ground squirrel closes the entrance to its burrow with an earth plug when it hibernates and sometimes when it retires for the night.

ID: head and front of shoulders are rich chestnut brown; buffy white eye ring is broken toward the ear; 2 black stripes on either side of a white stripe run along each side, from top of shoulder to hip; back is grizzled gray; lighter undersides; tail is blackish above with cinnamon buff sides
Length: 11–13 in (28–33 cm)
Weight: 6–12 oz (170–350 g)
Habitat: open coniferous forests on mountain and foothill slopes up to alpine tundra
Diet: green vegetation, fungi, seeds, fruits, insects, carrion in summer; conifer seeds are a major component of fall diet
Similar species: chipmunks (pp.110–119)

On talus slopes, these ground squirrels are found alongside pikas. Both small mammals issue high-pitched cries, continually appearing and disappearing among the boulders.

At close range, you can often see their bulging cheek pouches crammed with seeds and other food, ready to be stored in their burrows.

These high-elevation ground squirrels are often mistaken for chipmunks. A closer look reveals a difference: the stripes stop short at this ground squirrel's neck; all chipmunks have stripes running through their cheeks.

Wyoming Ground Squirrel

Urocitellus elegans

This ground squirrel's eyes stick out far to the side, helping it to see predators flying above, such as hawks and eagles.

Once considered to be a form of the more northerly Richardson's ground squirrel (*U. richardsonii*), the Wyoming is now recognized as a separate species.

This animal spends much of the summer foraging and sunbathing, retreating to its burrow for midday siestas or during stormy weather.

ID: grayish buffy brown back; top of nose is pinkish or cinnamon; light eye ring; rump may have indistinct brown barring; sides and belly are yellowish in early summer, becoming grayer later in season; tail is grayish buffy to speckled black above and pale orange below
Length: 10–12 in (25–30 cm)
Weight: 10–14 oz (280–400 g)
Habitat: dry slopes with sandy, gravelly or silty soils and short herbaceous vegetation; sagebrush, montane grassland, talus slopes; southern Wyoming to northern Colorado, and eastern Idaho to southwestern Montana
Diet: green vegetation, especially sage and legumes in early summer; also forbes, grasses, insects and other invertebrates, carrion
Group name: colony
Similar species: Uinta ground squirrel (p. 106), Richardson's ground squirrel

Thirteen-lined Ground Squirrel

Ictidomys tridecemlineatus

The thirteen-lined ground squirrel is perfectly camouflaged in its prairie landscape. Its striped back blends well with the alternating pattern of sun and shade created by tall grass.

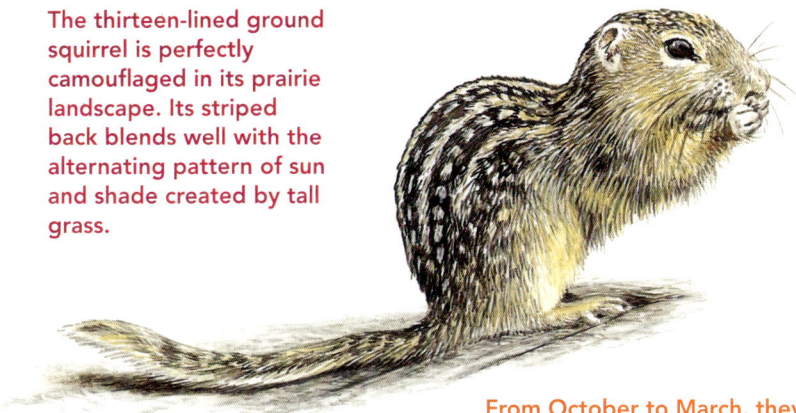

From October to March, they retire into their burrows, singly or communally, spending winter curled up into tight balls.

Highly social, these squirrels live in colonies and construct complex underground labyrinths to retreat to when threatened.

During hibernation, their respiration decreases from 100 to 200 breaths per minute to 1 breath every 5 minutes.

ID: brownish back has 13 alternately dotted and solid, buffy stripes; top of head is buffy, sprinkled with brown; buffy eye ring, nose, cheeks, feet and underparts; gray sides; thin, cylindrical, tawny tail; long, narrow head; large eyes; small ears
Length: 8¼-12 in (21-30 cm)
Weight: 2¾-8¼ (80-235 g)
Habitat: prairie, abandoned fields, mowed lawns, agricultural areas, edge habitats
Diet: mostly seeds; insects, slugs, other invertebrates; eats more small animals, including young birds, mice and carrion, than other ground squirrels
Group name: colony
Similar species: Wyoming ground squirrel (p. 104)

Uinta Ground Squirrel

Urocitellus armatus

Uinta ground squirrels hibernate for most of the year. Adult males enter hibernation as early as mid-July and may remain dormant until they emerge in April or mid-May.

ID: head, front of face and ears are cinnamon, with gray highlights on crown; sides of neck and face are pale gray; light buffy eye ring; cinnamon buff back; dorsal hairs have light pinkish buff tips; pale sides, feet and belly are pinkish buff to white; tail looks dark with gray underside
Length: 11–12 in (28–30 cm)
Weight: 10–15 oz (280–430 g)
Habitat: sagebrush grasslands, field edges and subalpine meadows; generally avoids dry, shortgrass prairies; nearly always above 5200 ft (1580 m), truly an inhabitant of mountains and high plateaus
Diet: omnivorous diet includes seeds, insects, forbs, some small vertebrates
Group name: colony
Similar species: Wyoming ground squirrel (p. 104)

Yearling males have the longest active season, spending 97 days above ground before entering hibernation, while juveniles are active for only 55 days.

Although they sometimes sit upright, these ground squirrels more often lie motionless, feeding in one area for some time before rushing to a new area to begin feeding again.

Where food is abundant, these ground squirrels live in large, dense colonies and excavate complex burrow systems to house all members of the colony.

White-tailed Prairie Dog

Cynomys leucurus

Easily identified by their white-tipped tails, these prairie dogs occur in great numbers in the sagebrush plains of Utah, Wyoming and Colorado.

ID: yellowish buff nose and back; prominent blackish-brown patches above each eye and on each cheek; pale cinnamon ears; black tipped guard hairs create a banded or speckled appearance on back; black claws with light tips; tip of tail is white
Length: 13-16 in (33-40 cm)
Weight: 1 1/2-2 3/4 lb (680-1250 g)
Habitat: dry mountain valleys and sagebrush grasslands at high elevations
Diet: leaves, stems and roots make up most of diet; also eats insects and carrion
Group name: coterie, colony, town

Prairie dogs are highly social, diurnal rodents that form large burrowing colonies. Younger animals live on the periphery of the colony and dominant ones live at the core.

Sentry guards scrutinize the surrounding land and sky for danger, while the rest of the colony forages, sunbathes, grooms or plays. A series of loud yaps warning of danger causes the entire colony to vanish underground.

Prairie dogs occasionally share their dens with western rattlesnakes, Great Basin gopher snakes and burrowing owls.

Least Chipmunk

Neotamias minimus

The sound of scurrying among leaves, a flash of movement and sharp, high pitched "chips" usually mean a least chipmunk is nearby.

This cute, curious rodent is the smallest of our chipmunks.

ID: gray belly and nape of neck; 5 brown-edged dorsal stripes with 2 extending onto head; tail is pale orange underneath
Length: 7-9 in (18-23 cm)
Weight: 1¼-2½ oz (35-72 g)
Habitat: wide variety of areas, including campgrounds, coniferous forests, sagebrush flats, alpine areas
Diet: berries, nuts, seeds, grasses, mushrooms, some insects
Similar species: golden-mantled ground squirrel (p. 102), red-tailed chipmunk (p. 112), yellow-pine chipmunk (p. 114)

Least chipmunks spend little time in high trees. They prefer the ground, where they bury their food and dig golf-ball sized entrances to their networks of tunnels.

The many western chipmunk species can be difficult to tell apart, but populations are separated by different habitat preferences. Least chipmunks are highly adaptable and will live just about any place not already occupied by another species of chipmunk.

Red-tailed Chipmunk

Neotamias ruficaudus

The most arboreal (tree-dwelling) of the chipmunks, this species builds well-insulated ball-shaped nests in trees or on the ground using dried grasses.

ID: large chipmunk; 3 dark and 2 light stripes on face; 5 dark and 4 light stripes on back; dark gray rump; rufous shoulders and sides; bright orange or rust-colored underside of tail
Length: 9-10 in (23-25 cm)
Weight: $1\frac{7}{8}$-$2\frac{1}{2}$ oz (53-72 g)
Habitat: dense, subalpine spruce-fir forests
Diet: conifer seeds, nuts, some berries, insects; sometimes feeds on eggs, fledgling birds, young mice, carrion
Similar species: least chipmunk (p. 110), yellow-pine chipmunk (p. 114)

When it is not defending its territory or hiding from predators, this chipmunk collects, caches and eats seeds or often performs charming sun- and soil-bathing antics.

The red-tailed chipmunk defends its territory with a warning bark.

Yellow-pine Chipmunk

Neotamias amoenus

ID: distinct dorsal stripes alternate: 5 dark and 4 light; 3 dark stripes on each cheek with middle stripe through eye
Length: 8-9 in (20-23 cm)
Weight: 1 5/8-3 oz (46–85 g)
Habitat: open coniferous and montane forests, forest edges, burned sites up to treeline
Diet: mostly conifer seeds, nuts, some berries, insects; also eggs, fledgling birds, young mice, carrion
Similar species: least chipmunk (p. 110), red-tailed chipmunk (p. 112)

Perhaps more common in the mountains than the wide-ranging least chipmunk (p. 110), the yellow-pine chipmunk can be seen by anyone who is willing to invest the time and effort in a search. Look for them dashing in and out of rocks and vegetation.

Watch for yellow-pine chipmunks in open forests of...yellow pines (Ponderosa pine)!

Flowing bushy tails, striped faces and backs, and bursting, round cheeks filled with seeds all characterize these endearing Rocky Mountain chipmunks.

Uinta Chipmunk

Neotamias umbrinus

ID: medium-sized chipmunk with alternating dark and light stripes; dark stripes are usually brownish; brown flanks, shoulders and head; black-tipped tail; outermost stripe is white, bordered by brown, not black
Length: 8-9 ½ in (20-24 cm)
Weight: 2-3 oz (57-85 g)
Habitat: subalpine coniferous forests and rocky slopes up to treeline
Diet: mostly conifer seeds, nuts, berries; also fungi, mushrooms, insects
Similar species: least chipmunk (p. 110), Colorado chipmunk (p. 118), yellow-pine chipmunk (p. 114)

The Uinta chipmunk prefers mature lodgepole pine stands with an open understory and rocky ground surface. It is typically solitary and relatively silent.

This tree-dwelling chipmunk can be found in high elevation habitats similar to those occupied by the red-tailed chipmunk (p. 112) farther north.

This chipmunk puts on a large layer of fat to support itself through its winter hibernation.

Colorado Chipmunk

Neotamias quadrivittatus

Chipmunks tend to scatter their food among several cache sites, increasing their chances of saving some food from the thievery of other animals.

ID: a pattern of alternating dark (mostly black) and light stripes extends from tip of nose to rump; fur is yellowish-gray to chestnut on sides and lighter below; lowest, pale stripe is bordered by a small black stripe
Length: 8-9½ in (20-24 cm)
Weight: about 2 oz (57 g)
Habitat: coniferous forests, alpine tundra, chaparral grasslands
Diet: mostly vegetation, including pinion nuts, acorns, spruce seeds and fungi; also insects, bird eggs, nestlings
Similar species: Uinta chipmunk (p. 116), least chipmunk (p. 110)

The Colorado chipmunk, like most of its relatives, is often seen scampering across open areas or roads with its tail held vertically.

Chipmunks sometimes eat eggs and nestlings of small birds, climbing high into trees to obtain these protein-rich foods.

Colorado chipmunks must not only store large quantities of food, but they must also accumulate enough insulative body fat to protect them from the bitter cold.

Red Squirrel

Tamiasciurus hudsonicus

Intruders beware! This fearless, extremely vocal tree squirrel may chatter, stomp its feet, flick its tail and scold you with a piercing cry until you flee from its territory.

ID: short fur is rusty-red to olive-brown; white undertail; white eye ring; black whiskers
Length: 11–13 in (28–33 cm)
Weight: 6–11 oz (170–310 g)
Habitat: coniferous and mixed forests at various elevations; common in towns, ravines
Diet: conifer seeds; also flowers, birds, berries, mushrooms, eggs, mice, insects
Similar species: Abert's squirrel (p. 124), northern flying squirrel (p. 122)

Red squirrels do not hibernate and must store massive amounts of food for winter. Mounds of discarded pine cone scales are evidence of their winter caches, called *middens*.

Red squirrels feed on pine cones like they are eating corn-on-the-cob.

These squirrels are ready to mate in spring. Their courtship involves daredevil leaps through the trees and chases over the forest floor.

Northern Flying Squirrel

Glaucomys sabrinus

Northern flying squirrels may be just as common in an area as red squirrels (p. 120), but their nocturnal activity patterns mean they are rarely seen. Flying squirrels may routinely visit bird feeders at night.

ID: a web or fold of skin extends from ankles to wrists; large dark shiny eyes; light brown back with hints of gray; light gray to cinnamon underparts; noticeably flattened tail
Length: 9 1/2–14 in (24–36 cm)
Weight: 2 5/8–6 1/2 oz (74–185 g)
Habitat: primarily old-growth coniferous and mixed forests
Diet: mainly lichens, fungi; also buds, berries, seeds, arthropods, bird eggs, nestlings, conifer cones
Similar species: red squirrel (p. 120)

Long flaps of skin (called the *patagium*) stretched between the forelimb and hindlimb and a broad, flattened tail allow the northern flying squirrel to glide swiftly from tree to tree.

After emerging from its tree cavity nest, this squirrel floats down to the forest floor and feeds on a variety of food, including mycorrhizal fungi. Through its stool, the squirrel spreads the beneficial fungus, helping both the fungus and the forest plants.

Abert's Squirrel

Sciurus aberti

With long ear tufts and a broad, plumed tail the Albert's squirrel is one of the easiest squirrels to identify in the southern Rockies. It is also called the tassel-eared squirrel.

ID: large squirrel with conspicuous, long, tasseled ears; long, bushy tail is outlined in white; whitish undersides; light phase is gray on back with a black stripe on each side of a white belly and a gray tail; dark phase is uniformly dark black or brown and is found in northern Colorado
Length: 18–23 in (46–58 cm)
Weight: 24–32 oz (680–910 g)
Habitat: ponderosa pine, piñon-juniper forests
Diet: main foods are pine cones, the sweet inner bark of pine twigs, pine buds and fungi that grow on or around trees
Also called: tassel-eared squirrel
Similar species: red squirrel (p. 120), northern flying squirrel (p. 122)

This handsome tree squirrel builds an elaborate all-season nest in the crotch of a ponderosa pine, where it raises young and finds shelter during cold or wet weather.

From March to April, females entice several males to engage in a chase through the trees before selecting a mate.

Kaibab squirrel

This squirrel has both a light and a dark color phase. A handsome subspecies, known as the Kaibab squirrel, has a totally white tail and lives only on the northern rim of the Grand Canyon.

Rock Squirrel

Otospermophilus variegatus

ID: back is mottled grayish to blackish-gray; shoulders are darker; sides and upper surfaces of feet are brownish; belly is light grayish-brown; bushy tail is rarely as long as body
Length: 17-21 in (43-53 cm)
Weight: 21-28 oz (600-790 g)
Habitat: rocky canyons, cliffs, talus slopes, boulder fields, roadside slopes
Diet: a wide variety of seeds, fruits, nuts, plants

With its long, bushy tail, the rock squirrel looks a lot like a tree squirrel. More so than other ground squirrels, it is an agile climber that often seeks out berries and seeds in trees or shrubs.

Rock squirrels live in large colonies with a distinct social order. Females form maternal groups around main burrowing sites. These colonies are aggressively defended by adult males.

True to its name, this squirrel inhabits rocky areas. It is usually active at twilight.

American Pika

Ochotona princeps

ID: reddish or grayish-brown coat with gray undersides; large, rounded ears; beady black eyes; long whiskers; no external tail; front and rear legs are nearly equal in length, so pikas run instead of hop

Length: 7–8 in (18–20 cm)

Weight: 5–11 oz (140–310 g)

Habitat: rocky talus slopes and rocky fields at higher elevations in mountains

Diet: varied; a wide variety of vegetation found near its rocky shelter, including broad leaved plants, grasses, sedges

Similar species: bushy-tailed woodrat (p. 76)

The American Pika lives in rocky landscapes high in the mountains. This busy creature scurries in and out of rocky crevices, issuing its warning PEEEK! call and gathering succulent grasses.

Pikas carry bundles of grass in their mouth, piling the vegetation on sun-drenched rocks to dry before storing it for winter food.

The rambunctious, spirited pika looks like a rodent, but it is more closely related to rabbits and hares.

Snowshoe Hare

Lepus americanus

summer coat

ID: *In summer:* coat is rusty brown above; crown of head is darker and less reddish than back; chin, belly and lower surface of tail are white; adults have white feet; immatures have dark feet. *In winter:* coat is white except ear tips remain black
Length: 15–21 in (38–53 cm)
Weight: 2–3 lb (0.9–1.4 kg)
Habitat: various; found almost everywhere there is forest or dense shrubs
Diet: a wide variety of grasses, forbs, shrubs in summer; mostly buds, twigs, bark of willows and alders in winter; also eats carrion
Similar species: white-tailed jackrabbit (p. 134), black-tailed jackrabbit (p. 132), mountain cottontail (p. 136)

The snowshoe hare has several fascinating adaptations for winter, including large, snowshoe-like hindfeet and a coat that changes color with the seasons.

A snowshoe hare's coat is brown in summer. In response to shortening day lengths as winter approaches, the hare's coat changes to white winter camouflage. Hares have no control over this transformation, and if the first snowfall is late, their white coats are highly visible.

Large hindfeet allow the hare to cross soft snow, rather than sinking into the powder. Unfortunately, this is minimal help against the equally big footed Canada lynx, a specialized hunter of the snowshoe hare.

Black-tailed Jackrabbit

Lepus californicus

Unlike its white-tailed cousin, the black-tailed jackrabbit does not turn white in winter.

ID: peppery brown overall; a black stripe runs down its back; very long ears with black tips; very long front and rear legs
Length: 20–24 in (51–61 cm)
Weight: 5–10 lb (2.3–4.5 kg)
Habitat: lower-elevation shrublands, sagebrush, fields, meadows, farmlands
Diet: a wide variety of green plants in summer, especially elf alfalfa; dried and woody plants in winter
Similar species: white-tailed jackrabbit (p. 134), snowshoe hare (p. 130)

Black-tailed jackrabbits can be easily identified by their huge ears. The long ears release excess body heat, helping these hares stay cool in their hot, arid habitat.

This hare spends much of its day crouched in a form it scratches out of the ground. At dawn and dusk, it can often be seen grazing at roadsides.

These speedy animals can run up to 40 mph (64 km/h), faster than a car drives in the city! They can also leap 15 ft (4.5 m), the length of 3 park benches.

White-tailed Jackrabbit

Lepus townsendii

summer coat

ID: *In summer:* light grayish-brown back; nearly white undersides, hindfeet and tail. *In winter:* entire coat turns white except for grayish forehead and black ear tips; tail is quite long and held rigidly when jackrabbit runs
Length: 21–25 in (53–64 cm)
Weight: 6–12 lb (3–5.4 kg)
Habitat: open woodlands, grasslands, shrublands, sagebrush
Diet: commonly eats grasses and forbs, also alfalfa and clover in agricultural regions; shrubs and weedy plants are added to diet in winter
Similar species: black-tailed jackrabbit (p. 132), snowshoe hare (p. 130)

Jackrabbits are not rabbits, they are hares. Unlike rabbits, which give birth to helpless young and hide from danger, hares give birth to precocial young and try to outrun predators.

This hare is capable of running 45 mph (72 km/h) in short spurts. Before taking flight, it sits motionless with its ears laid flat over its back.

The lean white-tailed jackrabbit is the largest and most encountered hare in much of the Rocky Mountains and prairies.

Mountain Cottontail

Sylvilagus nuttallii

ID: dark, grizzled, yellowish-gray upperparts; whitish underparts; rusty orange patch on nape of neck; front and back edges of ears are white; ears are usually held erect when the rabbit runs; tail is blackish above and white below
Length: 13–16 in (33–40 cm)
Weight: 1½–2¼ lb (680–1020 g)
Habitat: a major habitat requirement is cover, whether brush, fractured rock outcrops or buildings; prefers edge habitats where trees or brushy areas meet meadows or agricultural land
Diet: grasses, forbs; in many areas they feed heavily on sagebrush and juniper berries
Also called: Nuttall's cottontail

This cottontail fits the image of the classic cute bunny, but the plush-toy appearance masks a tough animal that can survive in a harsh, unforgiving landscape full of predators.

As the sun sets, cottontails emerge from their daytime hideouts to graze on succulent vegetation. They daintily nip at grasses, always just a short leap from dense bushes or a rocky shelter.

Mountain cottontails spend most of their days sitting quietly in dug-out depressions, called *forms*, beneath vegetation or under rocks, boards, abandoned machinery or buildings.

Long-eared Myotis

Myotis evotis

ID: upperparts can vary from light yellowish-brown to dark brown; underparts are lighter; black ears are $^3/_4$ in (2 cm) long with a long, narrow tragus; wings are mainly naked; only lower fifth of tail membrane is furred; calcar is keeled

Length: $3^1/_2$–4 in (9–10 cm)

Wingspan: 11 in (28 cm)

Habitat: in many habitats, wherever there are suitable roosting sites; commonly found in forests, shrublands, grasslands, agricultural areas; roosts in buildings, under tree bark, occasionally in caves; hibernates in caves, mine adits

Diet: moths, flies, beetles, spiders

Group name: colony, cauldron

Also called: long-eared bat

Similar species: all myotis species are generally indistinguishable in the field

Like all other Rocky Mountain bats, this bat uses echolocation to navigate and find prey in complete darkness.

By producing short bursts of high frequency sound, then listening for the echo bouncing off objects in the distance, bats can determine the direction, distance, size and texture of objects to avoid or eat.

For the long-eared myotis, feeding peaks at about 30 minutes after full darkness, somewhat later than most other bats.

Little Brown Myotis

Myotis lucifugus

These wide-ranging, common bats are quite likely the first bat most people encounter.

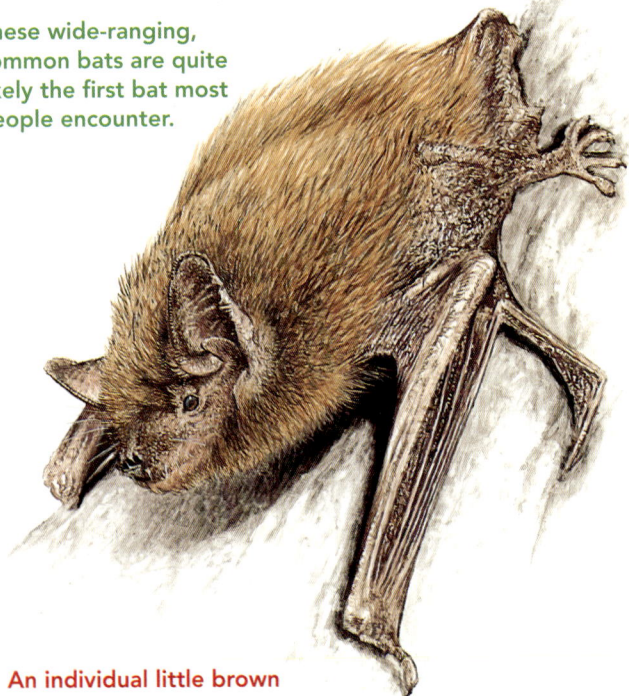

An individual little brown myotis can eat 900 insects per hour. A typical colony may eat 45 kg (100 lb) of insects a year.

ID: small brown bat; color changes from light to dark brown on back; lighter underparts; wing and tail membranes are mainly unfurred; ears are ½ in (13 mm) with a bent tragus, half as long as ear; calcar is long and unkeeled
Length: 3–4 in (8–10 cm)
Wingspan: 9 ¾ in (25 cm)
Habitat: in many habitats at various elevations; roosts in buildings, barns, caves, rock crevices, hollow trees, under tree bark; hibernates in buildings, caves, mine adits
Diet: feeds exclusively on night-flying insects, especially new aquatic emergents
Group name: colony, cauldron
Also called: little brown bat
Similar species: all myotis species are generally indistinguishable in the field

These bats form large maternal roosting colonies each summer to give birth and raise young.

Virtually helpless at birth, a single offspring spends its first few days clinging to the chest of its mother until it is strong enough to remain at the roost site.

Yuma myotis

The Yuma myotis (*M. yumanensis*) is virtually identical but its range extendes farther south in the Rockies.

Hoary Bat

Lasiurus cinereus

**This beautiful bat is
an oddball among its
kind—both males and
females live solitary
lives, with females
usually giving birth
to 2 young.**

ID: large bat; grayish fur with white tips gives a heavily frosted appearance; throat and shoulders are toffee colored; ears are short, rounded and furred, with naked, black edges; tragis is blunt and triangular; upper surface of feet and tail membrane are completely furred; calcar is modestly keeled
Length: $4\,^{3}/_{4}$–$5\,^{1}/_{2}$ in (12–14 cm)
Wingspan: 15 in (38 cm)
Habitat: roosts on branches of coniferous and deciduous trees and occasionally in tree cavities
Diet: insectivorous; mainly eats moths, planthoppers, flies, beetles
Similar species: silver-haired bat (p. 144), big brown bat (p. 146)

Hoary bats roost in trees, not caves or buildings, and wrap their wings around themselves for protection against the elements.

At night, look for their large size and slow wingbeats over open terrain.

These bats often roost in orchards, but they are insectivores and do not damage fruit crops.

Silver-haired Bat

Lasionycteris noctivagans

This bat flies during twilight hours, patrolling open fields, water surfaces or treetops for prey. It often flies low to the ground, dipping and flopping about, catching insects.

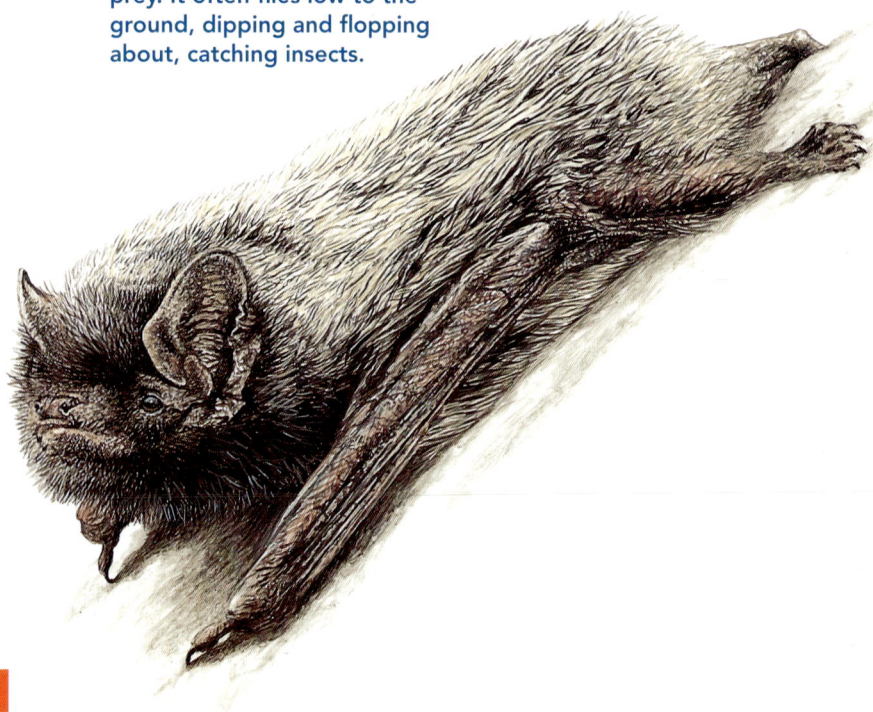

ID: fur is nearly black, with long, white tipped hairs giving a frosted appearance; naked ears and tragis are short, rounded and black; light covering of fur over entire tail membrane
Length: 3½–4¼ in (9–11 cm)
Wingspan: 12 in (30 cm)
Habitat: roosts in cavities and crevices of old-growth trees
Diet: feeds mainly on moths, foraging over standing water or in open areas near water
Group name: colony; cauldron
Similar species: hoary bat (p. 142), big brown bat (p. 146)

The silver-haired bat is similar to the hoary bat in its habit of roosting in trees, but it can be found in small, loose groups.

To conserve energy on cold days, it can lower its body temperature and metabolism—a state known as *torpor*.

Big Brown Bat

Eptesicus fuscus

The big brown bat is not abundant but is frequently encountered because of its tendency to roost in human-made structures.

ID: large bat; mainly brown with lighter underparts; fur appears glossy or oily; males are usually smaller than females; face, ears and flight membranes are black and mainly unfurred; blunt tragus is about half as long as ear; calcar is usually keeled
Length: 4–5 in (10–13 cm)
Wingspan: 13 in (33 cm)
Habitat: in and around human-made structures; easily adapts to parks, cities, farmlands; occasionally roosts in hollow trees and rock crevices
Diet: mainly beetles, planthoppers
Group name: colony, cauldron
Similar species: hoary bat (p. 142), silver-haired bat (p. 144)

An effective aerial hunter, the big brown bat's ultrasonic echolocation (80,000 to 40,000 hertz) can detect flying beetles and moths up to 16 ½ ft (5 m) away, about the length of a balance beam.

This bat flies above water, around streetlights and over agricultural areas searching for prey, which it scoops up with its wing and tail membranes.

It has been known to change hibernation sites midwinter, a time when it is extremely rare to spot a bat.

Townsend's Big-eared Bat

Corynorhinus townsendii

Endowed with relatively enormous ears, these bats catch night-flying moths and flying insects.

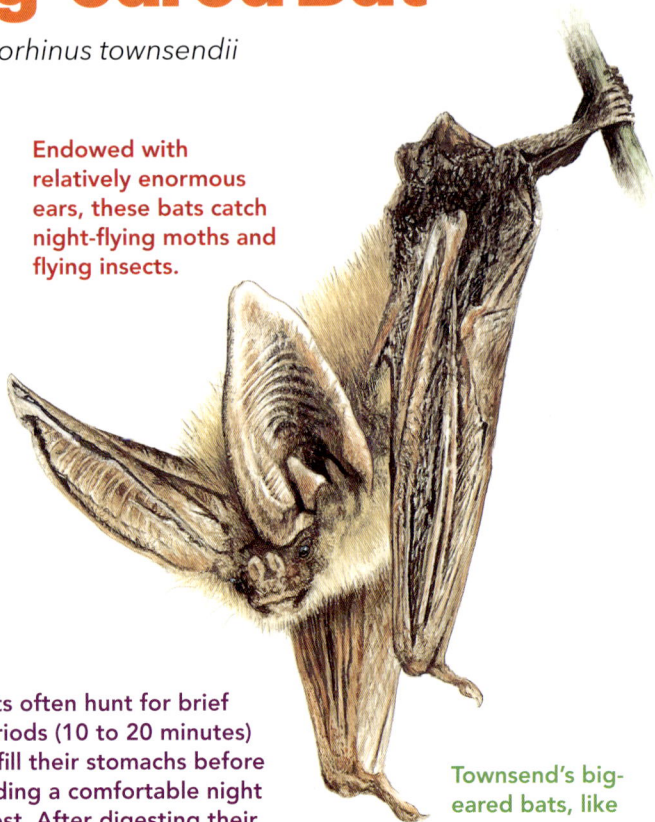

Bats often hunt for brief periods (10 to 20 minutes) to fill their stomachs before finding a comfortable night roost. After digesting their first meal, they alight again to hunt.

Townsend's big-eared bats, like most bats, are extremely sensitive to disturbance during winter hibernation.

ID: medium sized; brown overall with lighter underparts; large ears are half entire body length with a long, sharp tragus
Length: 3–4¼ in (8–11 cm)
Wingspan: 11 in (28 cm)
Habitat: open areas near coniferous forests and in arid areas; roosts in caves, buildings, old mines
Diet: mainly small moths; also beetles, flies
Group name: colony, cauldron
Also called: western big-eared bat

Spotted Bat

Euderma maculatum

The spotted bat is the rarest bat in North America.

Most bats vocalize beyond our hearing, but while feeding, this bat gives loud, high-pitched, metallic squeaks that are easily heard by humans.

These solitary bats seem to roost primarily in crevices on cliffs and stony outcrops.

ID: extremely long pinkish to light tan ears project forward in flight; black back; whitish belly; large white spot on each shoulder and on rump
Length: 4¼–4¾ in (11–12 cm)
Wingspan: 12 in (30 cm)
Habitat: highland ponderosa pine regions in summer; descend to lower-elevation desert areas in autumn
Diet: mostly noctuid moths; also beetles
Also called: death's head bat, jackass bat

Dusky Shrew

Sorex monticolus

Most of the heat energy shrews produce is quickly lost to the environment, and so shrews must eat their own body weight of food each day to maintain their internal body temperature.

Dusky shrews who go without food for more than a few hours will starve to death.

Shrews have an incredibly high metabolic rate, with heart rates often reaching 1200 beats per minute!

ID: brown back and sides; gray underparts. *In winter:* overall darker pelage
Length: 3½–5½ in (9–14 cm)
Habitat: wide variety of wet to moist habitats at various elevations up to alpine meadows
Diet: mainly adult and larval insects; also eats earthworms, spiders, snails, slugs, carrion, some vegetation
Similar species: pygmy shrew (p. 154)

Dwarf Shrew

Sorex nanus

This tiny shrew is about the length of a matchstick!

The entrance to its burrow is small, often no larger than the diameter of a pen.

Winds often sweep upslope, carrying insects and spiders with them. Dwarf shrews are most often found in ridges where these winds weaken, waiting for their next meal to drop in.

ID: brown back; gray underside; tail is dark above and light below
Length: $3^3/_8$–4 in (8.6-10 cm)
Habitat: montane regions of the eastern front ranges; beneath rock rubble in alpine regions, dry brushy slopes
Diet: larval insects, other soft-bodied invertebrates; immature shrews eat mostly vegetation, spiders
Similar species: pygmy shrew (p. 154)

American Water Shrew

Sorex palustris

The water shrew's larger size and specialized aquatic adaptations allow it to hunt small fish, tadpoles and aquatic invertebrates in cold ponds and streams.

This fierce predator swims well and dives after its prey. Large hindfeet, fitted with stiff, bristly hairs, act as flippers.

When water shrews dive, air bubbles trapped in their thick fur transform them into sleek torpedoes. To return to the surface, they simply stop swimming and the buoyancy of the air pops them back up to the surface.

ID: coat is dark, velvety brown to black with whitish-gray undersides; large hindfeet fitted with stiff, bristly hairs; distinct bicolored tail
Length: 5–6½ in (13–17 cm)
Habitat: lakes, ponds, marshes, streams with vegetated shorelines
Diet: aquatic insects, spiders, snails, other invertebrates, small fish
Also called: northern water shrew, common water shrew

Arctic Shrew

Sorex arcticus

The Arctic shrew's coat changes seasonally, which is unusual for a shrew.

summer coat

Its winter coat is longer and denser than its summer coat, and it is also more vibrant with its coal black back and white belly.

ID: gray-brown sides, cinnamon-colored tail. *In summer:* chocolate brown back; grey underparts. *In winter:* glossy black back; white undersides
Length: 4-4 ¾ in (10-12 cm)
Habitat: moist areas in boreal forest or along its edges; also open areas, dried-out sloughs, streamside habitats among shrubs
Diet: mostly larval and adult insects; also earthworms, snails, slugs, carrion
Also called: saddle-backed shrew

Pygmy Shrew

Sorex eximius

Watch for this shrew's constantly twitching snout as it hunts for insects and carrion, and keep your nose tuned for its strong, musky odor.

Pygmy shrews may consume more than three times their own body weight in food each day to survive. All shrews are insectivores.

The pygmy shrew is the smallest of all North American mammals.

ID: reddish to grayish-brown overall, with lighter underparts; tail is usually less than 40 percent of shrew's total length. *In winter:* usually grayer overall
Length: 2 3/4–4 in (7–10 cm)
Habitat: various habitats, moist to dry, and forested to open, including spruce-fir forests, bogs, wetlands
Diet: mainly adult and larval insects; also eats earthworms, nails, slugs, carrion
Similar species: dwarf shrew (p. 151)

Desert Shrew

Notiosorex crawfordi

The desert shrew does not need to drink water. It gets enough water from the food it eats.

It may be tiny, but this shrew is a fierce predator. It will take on animals bigger than itself, including scorpions.

This shrew is easy to indenify because of its conspicuous ears.

ID: grayish brown overall with light grey underparts; conspicuous ears
Length: 3-3½ in (8-9 cm)
Habitat: arid environments, such as deserts or sagebrush flats, especially in areas with prickly pear cactus or dwarf shrubs
Diet: insects, other invertebrates
Also called: Crawford's gray shrew; Crawford's desert shrew

Glossary

arboreal: living in or pertaining to trees

buff: a dull, brownish yellow

cache: a place in which food is hidden for future use; food hidden in such a place

calcar: in bats, a small projection from the inner side of each hind foot into the membrane between the hind legs

cambium: a layer of tissue under the bark of a tree from which new growth develops

carnivorous: flesh-eating

cecum: a pouch in the large intestine containing bacteria that digest cellulose

cervid: a hoofed mammal of the deer family (Cervidae)

colony: a group of animals living together and interacting socially

coniferous: pertaining to needle-leaved, cone-bearing trees (e.g., fir, spruce, pine)

deciduous: pertaining to trees that shed their leaves in autumn (e.g., oak, maple, elm)

dormant: a state of inactivity, with greatly slowed metabolism, respiration and heart rate

dorsal: pertaining to the back or spine

echolocation: the ability of some animals (including bats and cetaceans among mammals) to detect an object by emitting sound waves and interpreting the returning echoes, which are changed from bouncing off the object

endangered: facing imminent extirpation or extinction

extinct: no longer in existence anywhere

extirpated: no longer found in a given geographic area but still in existence elsewhere in the world

family: a biological classification that ranks below order and designates a group of closely related genera

forb: a nonwoody, flowering plant other than a grass

form: a shallow depression dug by a rabbit or hare in which to rest and hide

genus (pl. genera): a group of closely related species

granivore: a creature that eats grain

gregarious: preferring to living in large groups with other individuals of the same species; sociable

grizzled: having mostly dark fur that is sprinkled or streaked with grey or another light colour

guard hairs: long, coarse hairs that help protect a mammal's underfur from the weather

habitat: the environment in which an animal or plant lives

herbaceous: pertaining to plants that lack woody stems

herbivorous: plant eating

hibernaculum (pl. hibernacula): the den in which an animal hibernates

hibernation: winter dormancy

home range: the total area through which an individual animal moves during its usual activities (compare territory)

lanugo: the fine, soft hair that covers the body of newborn mammals

leveret: a young hare

marsupial: a group of mammals that bears live young that are born premature and develop in a pouch (e.g., opossums, kangaroos, wombats)

midden: a storage pile of conifer cones and seeds or a refuse pile of seed husks and cone debris on the ground

migration: the journey that an animal undertakes to get from one region to another, usually in response to seasonal and reproductive cycles

mustelid: a member of the weasel family (Mustelidae)

nocturnal: active at night

order: a biological classification that designates a group of closely related families of organisms

omnivorous: feeding on both plant and animal material

palmate: branching like the fingers of a human hand

patagium: a thin membrane that extends between the limbs and body of a bat or gliding mammal

pelage: the fur or hair of a mammal

predator: an animal that kills its prey (compare scavenger)

precocial: young born in a well-developed state and capable of moving and feeding independently almost right away

pronking: the bouncing gait of a deer or antelope in which the animal bounds and lands with all four legs simultaneously; also called stotting

rookery: a colony of breeding animals

rostrum: the snout of a whale or dolphin

runway: a beaten path made by the repeated travels of small animals

scavenger: an animal that feeds on animals it did not kill (compare predator)

species: a biological classification below genus that designates closely related organisms that are able to breed with them

territory: a defended area within an animal's home range

tine: a branch off the main central stalk of an antler

torpor: a state of dormancy in which an animal's metabolism and heart rate slow

tragus: a lobe projecting upward from inside the base of the ears, as in bats

treeline: the limit of normal tree growth as determined by elevation, temperature or other environmental conditions

tubercle: a small, rounded nodule on an animal's skin

underfur: a thick, insulating undercoat of fur

ungulate: a hoofed mammal

vibrissae: sensitive hairs or bristles ("whiskers") found on the face of a mammal and used in the sense of touch

Index

Distributed by: Canada Book Distributors - Booklogic
www.canadabookdistributors.com
www.lonepinepublishing.com
Tel: 1-800-661-9017

Title: Rocky Mountain mammals / Chris Fisher, Don Pattie, Tamara Hartson.
Names: Fisher, Chris, 1970- author. | Pattie, Don, 1933- author. | Hartson, Tamara,
1974- author.
Description: Includes bibliographical references and index.
Identifiers: Canadiana (print) 20230200613 | Canadiana (ebook) 20230200621 | ISBN
9781988183701 (softcover) | ISBN 9781988183718 (EPUB)
Subjects: LCSH: Mammals—Rocky Mountains—Identification. | LCGFT: Field guides.
Classification: LCC QL719.R63 F585 2023 | DDC 599.0978—dc23

Cover images: Ian Sheldon; MikeMareen; twildlife.
Image credits: AB Photography, 65; AllegressePhotography, 89; AndreAnita, 9; Anita Elder
Design, 31; Anne Lindgren, 125; Banu R, 31; Bebedi, 45; Betty4240, 37, 41, 69; bgsmith,
103; blagov58, 113; bloodua, 121; bobloblaw, 25; bywriter, 97; ca2hill, 115; Canis lupus, 65;
Carine Boekee, 111; Carol Gray, 63; Casey Wagner, 47; castigatio, 47; christiannafzger, 41;
ChristinaPrinn, 93, 101; Clayton Andersen, 53; cuphoto, 23; cwk15, 45; Dahrs, 57; Daniel
Friend, 69; Dave Malecki, 41; Dave Woodcock, 45; davidhoffmannphotography, 91; Dean_
Fikar, 95; Denisapro, 61; Denja1, 49; Dennis Stogsdill, 61; Diane Kuhl, 73; dmbaker, 9;
Drake Fleege, 93; erniedecker, 99; esmeraldaedenberg.jpg, 49; Fantasylmages, 63; Ferenc
Cegledi, 13, 99, 101; flownaksala, 15, 67; Fokusiert, 11; FotoRequest, 131; G Parekh, 127;
Gary Gray, 21; gatito33, 21, 51, 109; GatorDawg, 65; georgewinstonlee, 135; gjohnston-
photo, 19; Gregory S Phillipson, 47; Harry Collins, 19, 23; haveseen, 107; Harry Collins,
17; heckepics, 95; Henri Lehtola, 72; IPGGutenbergUKLtd, 27; Irina Babina, 135; James
Mutter, 127; janeff, 131; Jaroslav Sugarek, 17; JasonOndreicka, 147; jcrader, 129; jeu, 63;
Jillian Cooper, 39, 43, 55, 129; jkauffeld, 135; Jorge Figueiredo, 57; joshschutz, 11; Judith
Rawcliffe, 93; Juniperimages, 11, 29, 35, 39; Karel Bock, 35, 73; Kerry Hargrove, 125; Larry
Dallaire, 131; LeFion, 25; lorentrager, 55; Lynn_Bystrom, 27; M. Leonard Photography, 69;
MarcQuebec, 53; Matthew Jolley, 125; mdesigner125, 13; Michael-Tatman, 19, 59; Michel
VIARD, 95; MikeLane45, 29; mirceax, 67; mlharing, 13, 35, 39; moose henderson, 37, 51,
107, 137; mscornelius, 97; mtnmichelle, 63; mu_mu_, 115; Musat, 91; Nancy Strohm, 107,
109, 127; Nattapong Assalee, 99; PatrickHutter, 103; photographybyJHWilliams, 111, 117;
Piotr Krzeslak, 57; Christina Radcliffes 37; randimal, 97, 115, 137; Rex_Wholster, 103; Rip_
Hughes, 85; RobinEriksson, 49; RONSAN4D, 15; RT-Images, 101; seread, 31; slowmotiongli,
27, 29, 37, 55; Stefonlinton, 121; Steve_Gadomski, 55; SteveByland, 133; SteveClever, 39;
Straystone, 21; suesmith2, 137; T Schofield, 105; Timon Schneider, 121; twildlife, 15, 17,
21, 51, 133; VanH, 43; Viachaslau Mazai, 9; wayne stockburger, 11; Weber, 33, 75, 117, 119;
Rob Wijnsma 47; Wiktoria A Ciesielska, 117; Wirestock, 23, 47, 113, 133.

We acknowledge the financial support of the Government of Canada.
Nous reconnaissons l'appui financier du gouvernement du Canada.

Funded by the Government of Canada
Financé par le gouvernement du Canada | **Canadä**

Printed in China
PC: 38-1